PROFRESHIONAL

A GUIDE TO SURVIVING THE FRESHMAN YEAR OF YOUR PROFESSIONAL LIFE

Brooke Carter

ISBN 979-8-9851135-0-1

Cover design by Mahroo Sameen.

Editing by Patrick Price and Brooks Becker.

Printed in the United States of America.

First printing edition.

For more information, contact the author at:

www.brookecarterbrand.com

To anyone struggling to accept that
they are capable of great things
(both inside and outside of the workplace).

TABLE OF CONTENTS

INTRODUCTION

Starting a job, moving to a new place, graduating from college, or paying for your own health insurance are all huge milestones in your life. They are extremely difficult to navigate individually, much less when some or all of them are combined.

I moved to New York City immediately after my graduation from the University of Georgia to begin my first full-time corporate gig as a recruiter. The more fresh-faced professionals I met and befriended, the more a prevailing pattern emerged. Most new full-time professionals share a similar sentiment after joining corporate life for a few months: *This shit is significantly harder than I expected.*

Beyond feeling stressed and ill-prepared for the start of our full-time careers, everyone I spoke to felt like college and the people before us failed to mention how difficult the "life" part of working is. I know it sounds counterintuitive, there being a "life" part of work, but it's true—they didn't coin the phrase *work-life balance* for nothing. For the record, a more appropriate term would be *work-life clusterfuck.* Working on a full-time basis in itself is difficult and a great learning curve. But so is every other aspect you navigate off the clock—being the head of your own household, understanding health insurance, maintaining old

1

friendships, fostering new friendships, etc. The list goes on indefinitely.

These "life" challenges specific to young professionals are rarely mentioned to those just starting their careers. If or when they are, it's almost always exclusively in a context independent of work. But reality is quite the contrary. Work challenges and life challenges don't have strict boundaries. In fact, they frequently overlap—which means that young professionals enter corporate life unprepared for work challenges, life challenges, *and* the interaction between the two. Hence my earlier comment about *work-life clusterfuck*.

This brings up the famous question: *Was getting a degree even worth it?* Of course it was. Although my college degree has not allowed me to enter "The Real World" with the confidence and poise I thought it would, I can at least say I've done a nineteen-second keg stand in my lifetime (Where my state school folks at?).

But in all seriousness, degrees are not entirely obsolete. Individuals just need help filling in the gaps not taught at university, and to receive insight on what they-don't-know-they-don't-know when launching into a career. *Profreshional* was created for exactly that: guiding new members of the working world through all the chaos that starting a career may bring and (hopefully) helping them survive the experience with as little collateral damage as possible. It's intended to serve as a "heads up" to what you might run into within your first few years of employment in a corporate setting so you are not as caught off guard as I often found myself.

Before launching into the highs and lows, learning moments, real shit, and a plethora of head-scratching nonsense, it's important to give you a bit more background on who I am, and my perspective. After all, one of the major themes throughout this book is communication and *over-communication*, so I would be a hypocrite if I allowed readers to dive in headfirst without so much as an "FYI" to how I process the world around me.

I am a firm believer that our interactions as human beings are subjective. Rarely, if ever, are things black and white. How you perceive situations is a direct result of the experiences that have shaped you— and vice versa for all those you encounter. That said, here's a bit of background on the experiences that have shaped me into the bad bitch and sad bitch I am today (and directly impact how I think, act, and ultimately exist in the workplace):

- I was born and still identify as a female. My pronouns are she/her/hers.
- I was born in 1997 aka a member of Gen Z, baby! I'm on the cusp, so I still resonate with some of the millennial stereotypes (and memes). But yeah, I am undeniably a Gen Z-er. I used to cringe at this largely because of Tik Tok, but then I got a Tik Tok account, and developed a newfound respect for my younger GZ members.
- Myers-Briggs Type: ENFP. I take this personality type to heart and will defend the legitimacy of Myers-Briggs should you buck up at me and claim it's pseudoscience.
- I love to love. If you didn't pick up on it already, I am soft. I am sensitive. I am intuitive. I have struggled (still am?) to accept that. I've always hated it. I am a people person, people lover, and people pleaser, almost to a fault. I think this plays a large hand in how I process and respond to interactions with others, both inside and outside of the workplace.
- I have been working since the day I turned sixteen. Weirdly

enough, I've always loved it. Working is one of the only things I have ever felt good at.

- I was born and raised in South Georgia. Going to UGA was a "big move" for me, so naturally, post-graduation I had to find something even bigger (enter stage left, New York City).

Think of this book as your slightly seasoned best friend or marginally older sister. Treat it as a shoulder to cry on, if you will, because if you're anything like me, tears will play a leading role in the film that is *Adjusting to Adulthood and Corporate Life*. Revisit the relevant chapters during those moments of existential anxiety and dread, as they will be inevitable during this weird time. Come back to this text whenever you feel like giving up, and give it a read until you remember that you are a badass and that *you can do this*.

Let's normalize this surprising side of the Early Twenties coin. Although it does not align with the shiny Instagram Stories we share, many of us feel this way (and feel this way often). Revert back to where I say "It's OK" or "I understand and support you" or "You're empowered to feel this way," because I genuinely mean it.

Profreshional is intended as a source of support and affirmation during the moments you feel stressed beyond belief, overdramatic, totally alone, ready to cry, and completely crazy. Because I promise you, those moments will come.

This text is rooted in my opinion and personal experiences. I'd like to believe that I have taken an objective, thoughtful, and comprehensive approach to problem-solving; however, you may come to a different conclusion. Beyond the possibility for dissonance in our opinions of this book's messages, there may be dissonance in our opinion of *how* I deliver these messages. I have tried to remain true to who I am in this book, ensuring the tone of my writing accurately reflects how I analyze situations internally and how I would verbalize my story to those who care to listen in all its unfiltered, messy, sometimes sarcastic and coarse, yet ultimately sincere glory.

Yes, I will write "fuck," along with other words that may be considered profane. This will occur more than once throughout the course of this text. One of my favorite things my dad has ever said about me is "I was a sailor in the Navy for twenty-two years and Brooke swears more than I do." Why am I such a potty mouth? I don't know; I always have been. I think if we use curse words respectfully (not toward others) in common dialogue, it gives them less power. I just don't see casual cursing as a big deal (no disrespect to those who disagree).

I refrain from using profanity in totally inappropriate contexts, of course, as anyone should. But when it's just us adults here and we're all friends, I think a good drop of *"fuck this"* or *"for fuck's sake"* can be very effective.

I am also an idealist through and through. My appreciation for and practice of pragmaticism have increased as I've matured, but I still have a strong tendency to approach the world through an idealistic lens. However, I am extremely devoted to honesty and will put my idealist tendencies aside to ensure I am relaying honest information, especially throughout this text.

I'll share my experiences and advice with you in a realistic, no-bullshit fashion in hopes to protect and prepare other idealists like me. That said, it is important for you to know on the front end that some of the situations I recall are extremely frank, and may read as a *Debbie Downer* view on working full time. Let me assure you, I am not being pessimistic; I am being realistic. If you want to hold on to your naivety and beautiful, ignorant bliss as long as possible heading into your first full-time gig, I totally understand. Just know you may want to breeze through some of the latter chapters.

Lastly, *Profreshional* is organized in three applicable sections:

Part One: The First 90 Days covers a collection of tactical tips to utilize when you're just getting started. From navigating Outlook, to facilitating meetings, and everything in between, consider this section as a starter kit to help you dominate your onboarding program and blaze through the new hire learning curve.

Part Two: Everything Else details how "life happens" inside of the office, outside of the office, and the inevitable overlap between the two. We'll cover a collection of real-life scenarios new employees can anticipate and advice for how to navigate the aftermath.

And finally, Part Three: From the Masses offers a collection of others' perspective and advice specific to *their* Profreshional experiences. The purpose of this section is to combat the fact that my experiences may not be as relatable to some readers as they will be for others. My goal is for every reader to be able to walk away with something of value; by including messages from some of the most cherished members of my network, I believe *Profreshional* is one step closer to achieving that.

Ready for some welcome intel? Let's go.

PART ONE

THE
FIRST
90
DAYS

All the self-help books I've read and diets I've followed seem to follow a common theme of "90 days." It takes ninety days to build or break habits. People are most productive at work when they break up a project into ninety-day sprints. Employee onboarding within an organization actually takes ninety days (versus the measly four hours of orientation on your first day, like many of your fellow colleagues may think).

That said, assuming those studies are accurate, you have ninety days to land an impression with those around you—both with your direct team, as well as other members of the organization who are watching from afar. I don't say this to alarm you. In fact, I say it to inspire a bit of challenge and excitement. You have ninety consecutive days to show up to work and consistently ask questions, produce results quickly and effectively, act humbly, and demonstrate your enthusiasm to learn from the people around you. From there, you will earn the necessary street cred to make the remainder of your first year as a full-time employee infinitely more bearable.

By the time day ninety rolls around, your manager is thinking one of two things about you:

1.   *Best decision of my life! [YOUR NAME] has been such a big help.*

2.   *Oh my god. How much longer am I going to have to hold [YOUR NAME]'s hand?*

You don't want to fall into the second category. Because when you're in the second category, everything you do (or fail to do) moving forward is going to cause you exponentially heightened amounts of stress and anxiety.

When you're getting the vibe that your boss is not satisfied with you after your first three months of employment, dipping out to hit the gym during lunch is going to be stressful. Calling out sick (even if you truly are) is going to make you feel worse than the strep throat you may have contracted. Popping out for coffee mid-day because the shit in the café sucks, or leaving fifteen minutes early for happy hour is going to be more anxiety-inducing than your first day. All of these scenarios are commonplace for corporate employees, but if you feel like you have eyes on your back, even the smallest of slipups and slip outs will cause enormous amounts of guilt and anxiety.

You will know if your manager thinks you are incapable of delivering in your role. You will feel it; and once that impression is created, everything you do, no matter what you do, is subject to scrutiny. More than likely, any move you make will somehow manifest itself into becoming an artifact that contributes to "why things just aren't panning out." This is called negativity bias. Look it up.

While reversing a less-than-positive first impression is not impossible, it's significantly easier for you and everyone else involved to start things off on a strong foot. So how do we make sure your first few months of full-time employment go over well? How do we ensure your First 90 Days kick ass, leaving you and your teammates enthusiastic about the days ahead together?

HOW TO KICK ASS: THE BASICS

One of the most frustrating things I experienced during my first six months working a "big girl job" is the assumption by others that I know things I would have literally no way of knowing due to my tenure at the company. Let me elaborate by giving an example.

When you finally wrap up the first few days of slowpoke mode (aka getting software you need downloaded, creating usernames and accounts, finishing onboarding in whatever way that entails for your company, etc.), your manager and colleagues will be chomping at the bit for you to dive in and begin adding value to the team. In their eagerness, people often forget that you have never worked in this capacity with them, or really *ever before* in your life. So when a manager asks, "Hey so-and-so, did you already set up time with our compliance department like I mentioned for you to do three minutes ago?" your internal response will likely be something along the lines of: *No, I did not set up time with the compliance department for anything. One reason for that being that I'm not a mind reader and have no clue who our compliance department is. The other reason being that this is my second day I've ever had a full-time job in my life, therefore I do not even know how one goes about "setting up time" in Outlook.*

Your external response will likely be something along the lines of nervously sweating, apologizing quickly and asking your office neighbor how to "set up time." Buckle up, dear reader, because situations of this nature occur to infinity and beyond throughout employment. It's awkward when there is an assumption that you possess knowledge, skills, or task urgency that you would have no possible way of possessing. Your team will be eager for you to hit the ground running, and may at times forget that you're running at a much slower pace than they may be used to. Don't be scared to remind them that you're learning and unaware of how to do even the smallest of things they've just asked for (like sending a calendar invite).

But in hopes to help you hit the ground running, this section details the very baseline tactical tips I wish a fairy god person had given me as a newbie in the corporate world.

1.
MICROSOFT OUTLOOK

If you work for a super hip organization that uses G-Suite, I apologize in advance because not all of the following content may be applicable for you. For those who will be using Microsoft Outlook: Learn it, breathe it, live it.

GENERAL TIPS, STRATEGIES, AND OTHER SHIT TO LEARN

To help you get started, learn the intricacies of the program sooner than later.

ORGANIZE YOUR INBOX BY FOLDER

You likely will add/subtract/collapse as your role and responsibilities develop, but at the very least learn how to add folders so you are able to do so easily when the time comes. Searching for items in Outlook can be finicky, so putting in the extra effort to organize your messages by leveraging the Folders feature will save you an ample amount of time later on. Examples of types of inbox folders I have found most helpful are:

- **COMMUNICATION:** A catch-all folder that houses really anything sent to me by anyone outside of members of my department. This includes auto-notifications from updates made to Jira tickets, company-wide communication, etc.
- **"MANAGER NAME":** Obviously, this folder's title is my current manager's name—but that is confidential info, my friends. The point is to have separate folders for individuals who frequently delegate you tasks and projects. It could be your direct manager, as well as any key stakeholders you frequently interact with.
- **"TEAM NAME":** A similar idea as above. If you are in a position where you consistently support multiple teams, it may make sense to outline a folder for each group you serve. For instance, I currently support four different teams within my organization. Each have their own folders.
- **"KEY RESPONSIBILITY":** In your role you may not support specific teams, but you may consistently perform key tasks for a wide variety of teams/departments. If this is the case, it may be helpful to give each key area of responsibility its own folder. Let's say you are a business analyst who is responsible for managing data vendor partnerships, technical/product writing, and monthly reporting. You could create folders specific to each of the three job functions.

NEVER DELETE AN EMAIL EVER

No seriously, never. There is this fancy little function that Outlook has called "archiving" and it will save all folders within your inbox to a drive on your computer whenever your inbox gets full. The primary reason you should literally never ever delete anything in your inbox is twofold:

1. Saving your ass from yourself.
2. Saving your ass from others.

I am sorry to break it you so early in your career, but you will not be perfect. You will be messy, get confused, make mistakes, and blatantly forget entire conversations. You'll likely mutter *"oh shit, oh shit, of shit"* under your breath at least once per day, especially during your first six months of employment. Always having your previous dialogue on deck to refer back to will be crucial for you moving forward. And honestly, it can save you a lot of work if you find yourself performing repetitive or annual/quarterly tasks (copy and paste that email, baby).

Regarding saving your ass from others, I am not saying the people you work with are inherently evil. They likely will not intentionally throw you under the bus and giggle as they watch you fail. However, they too will be messy and get confused and make mistakes and blatantly forget entire conversations and mutter *"oh shit, oh shit, oh shit"* under their breath at least once per day. Meaning, you need to be armed and ready to reference previous threads of communication to un-drag yourself from that twelve-person email chain with the department head included.

LEARN HOW TO ARCHIVE YOUR EMAIL FOLDERS

I think the reason why is obvious now. It's located in the "Settings" panel.

RECALLING EMAILS

Recalling an email is slightly different than recalling a thought or memory. The function is not about *remembering* an email you've sent, rather it is about revoking it after you've realized, *oh shit, I shouldn't have sent that.* That said, teach yourself how to do this IMMEDIATELY. Learn how to recall emails *before* actually needing to do it. I have never felt adrenaline quite like the rush of the *oh fuck* moment when you hit send and simultaneously spot a spelling error, the wrong "John" included on the thread, forgotten attachments, someone else's name because you followed my "copy and paste" advice from above, etc. Sending an email and then noticing that it's incorrect (or sloppy) just after hitting send is terrifying. Like, life-flashing-before-your-eyes terrifying.

FLAGGING EMAILS

I didn't get into this habit until a few months in and wished I had used the "flag" feature since day one. It's hard to forget to accomplish something when it is red and glaring at you every time you scroll through your inbox.

OUTLOOK CALENDAR

On paper, the main functions of your calendar are to schedule meetings, block out large chunks of time to accomplish "deep work," and set reminders for yourself (and often others). However, your Outlook (or Google) calendar will soon become so much more than that. It will evolve into the guiding light of your life, comprised of key deadlines, important meetings, your grandma's birthday, your next dentist appointment, reminders to eat something so you don't forget and pass out at work—the list goes on. Learning how to do the basics (scheduling, etc.) before this grand evolution occurs will be important, so practice the below early on.

SCHEDULING MEETINGS

The rest is pretty straightforward once you learn how to schedule your first. Regardless, practice ahead of time how to create a new calendar event (which in corporate lingo can be referred to as "setting up time," "booking time," or "scheduling a meeting") and boom! Instant good impression left on members of your team.

MEETING INVITE TITLES

This can get awkward sometimes when you don't know how to phrase things, especially in instances such as pitching something with a leader within your organization. You can't go wrong with generic titles such as "Sync" or "Catch-Up" or "Quick Chat" with a more detailed message in the body of the invite.

MEETING INVITE BODY

Always have a message in the body of a calendar invite. And make sure it is thorough. This is a non-negotiable from my point of view. Trust me, the extra five minutes it takes to send a clear and thoughtful calendar invite is well worth it. You don't want to be known as the teammate who always puts random, wasteful, or unclear meetings on people's calendars.

If you need to book an urgent meeting and do not have time in the moment to draft a clear, concise message within the invitation, go ahead and schedule the time with a note that says "details to follow" within the calendar invite. Just be sure to circle back and update the invite with details as promised.

COLOR-CODE MEETINGS

Outlook provides a nifty little feature that allows you to color code different types of calendar events. I assume the purpose of this is to help individuals draw attention to very important meetings versus meetings that are simply BAU (business as usual). You can leverage this feature for your benefit in different ways. For instance, I have seen coworkers choose only one color and apply it to high-priority calendar invites, leaving everything else as the default color. This single color differentiation seems to suffice for most parties.

But if you're like me, you'll have a color assigned for every type of meeting that could possibly hit your calendar.

- **1:1 meetings:** Pink
- **Group meetings:** Blue
- **Presentations/Deadlines:** Yellow
- **Interviews:** Black
- **Fun/Personal:** Purple

Contrary to popular belief, my reasoning for this obnoxious, over-the-top organization is not due to having a type A personality. It is largely rooted in the fact that I am scatterbrained and this helps me understand what is on my plate for the day at a glance. And yes, also partially because I love the pretty colors. Whether you care to have your calendar look like a bag of Skittles or not, I do highly recommend having at least 1–2 colors (black or yellow stand out the most) for *really* important things that you do not want to overlook. Examples include key deadlines, presentations, or meetings where you are responsible for providing a deliverable.

2.
EMAIL ETIQUETTE

Maybe you love to communicate via text or Instagram DMs. Unfortunately, the corporate world isn't quite there yet, and still *loves* to conduct business over email. Although all channels I just mentioned can be considered "written communication," there are some very stark differences between writing an email and sending a DM to your favorite influencer. Even if most companies use email, norms for how they should be written will differ greatly from organization to organization. My best advice is to stick close to the phrasing and timing used by your manager and colleagues when crafting and sending emails. That said, I still want to share some best practices that are generally applicable and have helped elevate my writing game from "expert at text speak" to email savvy.

GENERAL SUGGESTIONS I FOUND HELPFUL WHEN WRITING EMAILS TO INDIVIDUALS AT ALL LEVELS

GIVE PEOPLE EVERYTHING THEY NEED, UP FRONT

This should be one of your key mantras as a young professional. Time is money and you sure don't want to label yourself as someone who wastes either one of them. Give people a break and provide as much information as possible on the front end. Do not make people look for things—especially your boss or other well-respected superiors. While it requires an insane level of discipline and diligence to accomplish this consistently, if you always structure your email updates and meeting invites with this mantra in mind, you will quickly set yourself apart from others in the most positive of lights. For example:

1. Are you planning to review an Excel sheet or PDF during the meeting you just scheduled? Attach both documents to the invite and be sure to refer the email/meeting invite recipients to it in the body of the email invite.

2. Are you referencing notes you took/published in your team's Sharepoint drive in an email reply to your boss? Hyperlink that sucker (and don't just copy/paste the link—replace text in line for cleanliness, using the "right click > link" function).

TO CC OR NOT TO CC, THAT IS THE QUESTION

When in doubt, cc it out! I wasted so much time during my early days stressing about whether I should "reply all" with a question or ping the person independently. I caused so much inefficiency by individually contacting people with similar, but slightly tailored messages because I was paranoid that I was sharing sensitive information with the wrong person. Nip these thoughts in the bud as soon as they cross your mind. You will save yourself an ample amount of time, energy, and stress-induced forehead wrinkles by changing your perspective of the "cc" email function early on.

Thanks to hilarious, yet somewhat toxic internet memes, I perceived cc'ing to have a negative connotation. We need to do our part in normalizing cc and breaking down the stigma. The feature gets such a bad rep, when in all actuality, it is one of the most useful tools for increasing transparency and streamlining communication.

CONCISION IS KEY

When leveraging a form of written communication like email, it is always important to get to the point as quickly and effectively as possible in your message. The actionable item or question you have should really be highlighted in the first 1–2 lines of text, otherwise you risk people getting lost in the context you're providing.

In my experience, this rule is even more applicable the higher up in the command chain the recipient is. The more senior an individual is within a company, the more responsibility they have, which entails more emails awaiting their review and response on a daily basis. You do not want to find yourself on the other side of TL/DR (too long, didn't read) when updating your manager on an important task or asking an urgent question. When concision in written communication is combined with the previous mantra "Give everyone what they need, up front," a powerful paradigm is formed. You will be unstoppable.

FIND YOUR EMAIL SIGNATURE

I know this may seem frivolous, but I think your email signature is an important first step in developing your brand as a professional. Finding your email "voice" will take time and surely evolve as you become more comfortable in your own skin as a professional, but I believe it all starts with determining how you want to sign your written communication. Sure, you can always switch up your signature when it feels appropriate to do so, but I have enjoyed picking one signature and sticking with it. That way any time my name appears in someone's inbox, they can fully expect the message to conclude with *"Many thanks, Brooke"*. It's a small way to personalize and own how you communicate with your colleagues.

3.
INSTANT MESSENGER

Yes, IM is different than email and therefore requires its own section for dos and don'ts. Again: Keep in mind that norms for written communication will differ from organization to organization, but I believe many of the below tips can be applied regardless of geographic location, position, and/or industry.

OFFICE BUDDIES

Even if you are someone who wants to keep a healthy boundary between your work friends and real friends, you will eventually find office buddies. If and when you do, you'll likely ping these people frequently on Skype, Slack, Teams, or some other form of messenger. This is great news! Office buds make the work day go by more quickly, so good for you for finding some. All organizations will likely harp on written communication during orientation, making you aware that all of it is tracked and recorded. This isn't a lie. Don't freak out though, because "tracked and recorded" is different than actively monitored.

But do know that every ounce of shit you might talk with an office buddy over IM will be there for future reference, god forbid it ever comes to that. Don't let this thought deter you from bonding with your teammates over the new firm-wide policy you hate, because those conversations can be very beneficial for building comradery and we'd all be liars if we said we didn't talk a bit of smack here or there with our office buddies. Just be mindful of to what extent you do it on company tools.

We will talk about establishing core values and tolerance thresholds later on, but this is a good first place to bring it up. Think about your personal threshold for what information you relay over corporate devices. Establishing where/when you might need to take your office gossip offline early on will be good for you, protecting you from possibly giving your firm really embarrassing read receipts. As common as it is to chat with your close colleagues over the company's IM, it is equally as common to take those close relationships to iMessage or WhatsApp too—so maybe save the most intense conversations for those apps rather than where your firm's IT team can see them.

TO PING, OR NOT TO PING

This falls in the category of "things you overthink/worry about and waste precious time and energy by doing so." Sometimes you really do need to hear from someone in order to move things forward. Since the Coronavirus pandemic in 2020, the use of IM tools such as Slack and Microsoft Teams has become increasingly normalized. Don't be nervous following up an email with a quick ping to flag something of high importance. It is possible for people to lose things, especially if they are in a role that inundates their inbox with emails.

JUST PICK UP THE PHONE

At a certain point, pinging back and forth on IM or email may not be the most effective way to talk through things. If you find yourself slinking down this path, don't be afraid to pick up the phone to quickly clarify what it is you need from your colleague. A quick five-minute phone call can often go a long way, especially when collaborating virtually, so don't be afraid to initiate it when you think it will provide efficiencies. I do recommend you summarize any conversation you have over the phone on existing email chains or IM chat threads. This provides a few key benefits:

- Ensures you understood the conclusion correctly and gives your counterpart the opportunity to correct anything you've summarized.
- Updates any observers in email chains on side conversations that were had, so they see the full picture.
- Provides a paper trail should you need to reference the date/time/details of the conversation at a later date.

YOU HAVE THE RIGHT TO REMAIN SILENT

When someone IMs you, you don't have to respond right away. And you don't have to respond at all if you don't want to. I don't know why it took me so long to come to this realization. I think people who are new to the workforce may fall victim to their eagerness to make a good impression and not realize that they are like any other member of this organization. You are within your rights to manage expectations, push back, and delay your response if necessary. Obviously, it may not be the best idea to blatantly ignore your manager when they are inquiring about an important project. You do you, but let's be clear that is not what I am empowering you to do here. What I *am* empowering you to do is:

- Leverage the "do not disturb" status feature if you are in the midst of an important task with an upcoming deadline. Don't feel the need to interrupt your deep work mojo just because someone IMs you.

- Don't feel that you need to monitor your work IMs or answer when you're on PTO (paid time off). There is power in fully disconnecting. Just ensure your status message informs people of when you'll be back online, so they'll know when they can expect a response.

- Ignore people who shouldn't be messaging you. If it's someone who is obviously riding way out of their lane (e.g., someone besides your manager trying to assign you work, someone who is being petty about a topic you don't prefer to engage in, etc.), you are allowed to disregard their message.

For most circumstances, however, disregarding IMs should not be a permanent solution. I encourage you to set a standard for your personal response time. And it can vary per stakeholder. For instance, I always like to respond to my manager ASAP. Even if I don't have the answer they need immediately, I will respond right away so they know I saw their request and will let them know when I plan to provide them with what they've asked for.

For key stakeholders or members of my firm's leadership team, I may follow a similar approach. For lower priority individuals and requests, I'll give myself a deadline of "by COB (Close of Business)." Since the nature of IMs is to be *instant,* I try to respond to everything by the end of that business day at the latest. Emails I give a bit longer of a response time threshold—typically 24–48 hours max response time depending on the nature of the message.

Establishing these boundaries for yourself and adhering to them from early on will not only help hold you accountable, but it will naturally help you organize/prioritize your tasks and stakeholder communication. You will organically develop a consistent pattern for your response times and your colleagues will eventually catch on. They will appreciate your consistency and reliability. It seems like such a small thing, but you'd be surprised how difficult it can be just to get someone to *reply* to your question or request. Making sure you aren't that guy is one of the quickest wins you can achieve for yourself.

4.
MEETING ETIQUETTE

There are two main types of meetings in the world: the ones you organize, and the ones you attend. It sounds counterintuitive but, from my experience, the earlier you are in your career, the more meetings you organize rather than just show up and attend. When you are new to your role and corporate life in general, you will need to prepare materials ahead of time regardless of which side of the meeting cookie crumbles.

Since day one of my career, very seldom have I found myself showing up to a meeting in which I can arrive just in the nick of time and kick my feet up (metaphorically) for the next 30–60 minutes. Instead, I am often frantically searching my files for the long list of pre-meeting notes I compiled along with pulling up the agenda and desired meeting outcome I sent around within the meeting's calendar invite, all while trying not to perspire in front of the other meeting attendees. It's as it should be, though. Because I know that showing up on time and over-prepared to every meeting are two seemingly small steps that can have an exponentially large impact in your career.

MEETING TYPES

You will quickly find that different types of meetings require different degrees of preparation, attention to detail, and seriousness. If it's a quick meeting to touch base on a project or talk through a problem with a peer, you can approach the session a bit more laxly. If it's a 1:1 weekly meeting with your manager, it's still a good idea to do some basic prep work and have a list of things to discuss on file.

SCHEDULING MEETINGS

When scheduling meetings, I have two key mantras:

1. Send invitations with a meeting agenda and desired meeting outcomes.
2. Prework each day keeps the inefficiency away. Always give prework! Always. It helps ensure a smooth and efficient conversation.

ASSUME YOU'RE FACILITATING UNLESS TOLD OTHERWISE

Nothing is more awkward than showing up to a meeting where nobody knows who is supposed to jump in first and lead the dialogue. In my early years of working, I have often found myself being asked to coordinate a meeting. I happily obliged and put something on the calendar. In my mind, however, I am not responsible for facilitating— I've just scheduled the thing. To avoid any awkwardness upon arrival to the meeting, be sure to clarify with the group ahead of time *who* is going to tee up the conversation. It may be as simple as pinging the tech lead who asked you to schedule the session in the first place to let them know you'll start the discussion by recapping the agenda you sent around and pass it over to them for the remainder of the dialogue. Taking the time to clarify this and set expectations will relieve both you and the tech lead of playing the game of emcee hot potato when the meeting begins.

TAKE NOTES FOR YOURSELF

Even if you weren't the notetaking type in college, you should strongly reconsider your habits now. I cannot tell you how many times I have thanked my lucky stars that I ended up jotting down something someone said or asked for.

I worked with a brilliantly talented technical project manager who shared with me a bit of advice that I'll now share with you. He keeps track of everything that he needs to do by using tiny red squares. Whenever he makes his to-do list for the day or week, he writes these items in red pen, with a tiny unfilled red box to start off each line item, so he can check it off when it's been completed. If he is in a meeting and assigned an action item ad hoc, he'll have his red pen on standby to write the task in the same format (line item led with an empty red box) so it stands out from the general notes he may have been jotting down. Every other day or so, he will flip back through his notebook and reconcile all the still incomplete little red squares into a new to-do list.

It seems incredibly manual, but I've tried it, and it is a magical strategy to ensure you don't let even the smallest of tasks slip through the cracks. These little red boxes have become part of his personal brand; his colleagues not only know that he will certainly get the job done and not forget what they've asked for, but they know that he will have a record of it. He's told me stories of colleagues from previous jobs ringing him to ask if he still had his notes from an important meeting years ago and if he remembered the outcome they decided on at the time. Because he archives these notebooks and has the little red squares there to track any action he was in charge of, he's been able to pull data from way long ago when needed.

This is a beautiful position to be in: people coming to you for record of key meetings because no one else is known for keeping as diligent notes as you do. I highly recommend adapting some version of the Tiny Red Box trick. Follow-through on tasks, no matter how big or small the project, will be critical while you are trying to make a positive impression. I have adopted the Tiny Red Box trick almost exactly as it was described to me, expect I swapped red ink for pink—because I love a good hot pink pen.

TAKE NOTES FOR EVERYONE ELSE

This concept will reap similar benefits to what we just discussed. However, the notes' style and application will look slightly different. When you take personal notes, you're documenting what *you* need to do in order to have your ducks in a row. But when you take notes for others, you're documenting everything that was said during a meeting (most importantly, capturing the action items), so *everyone else* has their ducks in a row. It's shocking how often people enter and leave a meeting without putting two words down on paper, which then astronomically increases the chances of them not delivering what was decided during the conversation.

When people fail to capture and complete their action items, things fall through the cracks, progress is delayed, conversations are repeated to remind people of what was supposed to be done, and time is wasted. We'll speak in detail later about how important it is to become The Expert They Didn't Know They Needed, or in other words, finding a way to become the single subject matter expert or point of contact for a critical workflow in your team.

As silly as it sounds, recording and archiving detailed notes during key meetings is a small way to make a big name for yourself within your team. Should you do this consistently and take notes of high quality, you'll quickly find that you become the go-to person for all sorts of information for key projects. In my experience, documentation is one of those "backlog tasks" that all teams find highly valuable and wish they performed more consistently, but often don't have the time (or dedicated resources) to accomplish in a systematic fashion.

For teams that do have somewhat of a system in place for recording and archiving conversations, more often than not there is room for improvement in how the notes are organized and circulated across teams. If you recognize a recurring meeting series goes undocumented, assume the responsibility of taking/distributing notes and key action points. You'll be invaluable!

5.
WFO VS. WFH

WFO (work from office) vs. WFH (work from home) has become an incredibly more interesting topic since the COVID-19 pandemic shook the corporate world and all the varying WFH policies that once stood within. As difficult as it may be to fathom, and as archaic as it may seem, many organizations did not have a formal WFH policy prior to March 2020 when COVID began to touch down in several countries around the world. Remote work and flexible work were concepts only the wokest of woke organizations normalized.

Suddenly, overnight, organizations all over the globe ditched all previous notions and skepticism around remote work and dove in headfirst. I am sure you're well aware of this timeline and event, as your academic institutions and/or jobs at the time were impacted and shifted. While by now you are probably a remote work and remote networking pro, it still feels appropriate to address the major differences between working in an office and working in the comfort of your home, from the comfort of your webcam.

As more individuals become vaccinated and cities, organizations, and national governments begin to reopen, companies are now faced with revisiting pre-pandemic policies regarding flexible working. I think that for every organization that plans to continue working in-office every day of the week, there is another company that will decide to adopt significantly more fluid requirements around in-office presence.

In my opinion, it is naive to think that after the one and a half years (and still counting at the time of this writing) of isolation and remote connection, things will bounce back to the exact same way they once were. That said, it is important to know the major differences of working remotely vs. working in-person and how to kick ass in both environments. I believe the key to successful performance regardless of the work environment is to identify the best practices of WFO and WFH and create hybrid habits that can be applied to both.

COMMUNICATION

When working in an office, organic "water cooler" dialogue is much easier to stumble across than when you are working remotely. This makes relationship building significantly easier to accomplish in an in-person setting than from behind the screens of your home devices. Similarly, business-oriented checkpoints are easier when in an office. If you have a quick clarifying question, you can pop over to someone's desk and ask for their assistance.

When you are strictly communicating virtually, you have the advantage of creating more paper trails than you otherwise might if you only worked in an office setting. "Quick questions" typically are asked over IM rather than shouting to your colleague the next desk over. If you are primarily communicating via IM or email, you have that thread of communication documented and ready to refer back to if needed. Having this archive of answers to my never-ending list of questions has saved me more times than I can count in the remote-working world.

MULTITASKING

I find that multitasking is much easier done in a remote setting than in-person. One of the beautiful things about all meetings being held over tools such as Zoom or Teams is the ability to share your screen for the meeting group using one monitor and manically type notes using another monitor. Depending on how tech-savvy your organization is and the resources they have available (e.g., distributing work laptops to all employees), you may have already had a similar luxury while WFO. But for those (like me) who brought an old-fashioned pen and paper to jot down notes during in-office meetings, the ability to take notes, format, publish, and distribute meeting minutes to attendees all before the meeting disbanded was a beautiful new way of working.

When working remotely, it is also much easier to get instantaneous feedback for time-sensitive projects or approvals from management for time-sensitive decisions. Because everyone is behind their computer screens simultaneously, everyone is multitasking. I have found it much easier to obtain swift approvals or have quick questions answered via IM rather than waiting all day to hear back like I might have done when working in-person.

TIME MANAGEMENT

As the entire global population is aware of by now, one of the major overarching themes of working remotely is "death by Zoom call." Because it's so much more difficult to foster organic collaboration and relationship building within fully remote organizations, people often see *"more Zoom meetings!"* as a solution. This then causes meeting calendars to become overscheduled and employees to experience a new phenomenon called "Zoom fatigue."

Time management becomes increasingly difficult when working from home for a variety of reasons, meeting-heavy calendars only being one of them. Since the pandemic and universal remote work began, work days have become busier, and in turn much longer. People spend more time online than ever, which makes it harder to manage the time within your overwhelmingly full workday to allow for an appropriate work-life balance. Not to mention when you work from home and home only, "the office" is defined by the same walls in which you live, eat, and sleep (making work-life balance all the more difficult to achieve). It's unfortunate how difficult it is to shut off from work psychologically when you do not have a physical commute embedded in your routine.

OVERALL PRODUCTIVITY

Whether or not employees are more productive when working in an office together or working from home is a total crapshoot in my opinion. Assigning blanket assessments is dangerous because productivity differs on a case-by-case basis. Which environment allows one employee to be more productive may be vastly different for another. Some people focus when they have the background noise of an open-concept office buzzing in their ear, whereas others prefer total silence. People who live in a house with enough square footage to have a proper home office might thrive in remote working. But people who live in NYC on an entry-level salary probably share an apartment and bathroom with multiple roommates and are forced to take calls from their bed since their private space is the size of other people's walk-in closets.

Not only is productivity extremely situational, it can fluctuate, especially when going from one extreme (working only from the office) to the other (working only from home). Too much of a good thing can easily become a bad thing, and I think society has seen that firsthand in the context of WFO and WFH.

For instance, what started for me as a spike in productivity because I was able to cut out in-office distractions, expand the length of my workday, and multitask during meetings, slowly diminished over time. I began to get burnt out, sick and tired of working in the confines of my four bedroom walls with less-than-ideal technology equipment, and the distractions of roommates (and my local coffee shop calling my name midday, tempting me to close the laptop for a quick cappuccino break).

BEST OF BOTH WORLDS

With governments and organizations slowly opening up across the globe, we are at a unique turning point where we will see more companies implementing a hybrid approach to workplace attendance. We've seen some CEOs, take JP Morgan for instance, demand all employees return to offices by a fixed date and if people have an issue with it, they can find a new job. Many other places, like Google, are taking a more flexible approach, now implementing a fixed number of "flex work days" into an employee's benefits package. These days are similar to PTO days, but allow employees to work from a remote location of their choosing for approximately two weeks out of each year.

Regardless of which team we are on or what organization we are a part of, I predict that most jobs and industries will begin to blur the lines between WFO and WFH. This means that you, as an employee, need to take note of the best parts of both worlds and begin to apply these strategies and ways of working to both environments. Your list of best practices will differ from mine depending on your role, industry, and company, but I've gone ahead and written a few down to get you started.

COMMUNICATION

- Continue being "paper trail" minded. If you discuss a project with your manager in the office during one of those watercooler moments, be sure to summarize it for your remote colleagues who might have missed the conversation. Updating IM groups or email chains as side conversations occur is always a best practice, whether the side dialogue happens in person or remotely.

- Consider virtual open office hours. These checkpoints can be set up for your team to join as needed, to receive clearance for tasks, remove blockers, or ask questions. They can also be leveraged for more social purposes, like catching up informally with colleagues or reviewing interesting articles they've seen recently.

- Adopt the mentality of "If you don't over-communicate, you're under-communicating." This is applicable for both WFO and WFH. Just as it's easy to book too many Zoom meetings to compensate for not having interaction in-person, it's easy to book too few checkpoints when your team begins working in the office more frequently. Make like Goldilocks and find what balance is *just right* for you, your team, and your boss. I always recommend scheduling recurring meetings so the time is there if you need it, but checking in ahead of time to see if there are topics to discuss or if the attendees prefer to cancel this time around.

MULTITASKING

- Identify what meeting structures enable you or your teammates to continue having meeting minutes signed, sealed, and delivered in a timely manner. If it means having someone else pull up the agenda during an in-person meeting and you sitting next to them typing away feverishly since you cannot do both at the same time, like you would during a remote meeting, so be it. Be upfront with your team and manager about the behavior change that needs to occur in order to reap the same efficiencies in person as you do while everyone works from home.

- If you are someone who needs quick responses or approvals from your manager who typically spends their workday in back-to-back meetings, going back to WFO might pose a challenge here, as checking your phone for messages may come across as "rude" during face-to-face meetings. If this sounds like a hurdle you may face, find a way to schedule in some time for your boss to check IM throughout the day so they can remove any blockers that might come up. Whether this is an agreement for them to check their email at a fixed frequency, permission to pull them out of meetings if absolutely necessary, or something else, find a way to continue that streamlined communication even when you both no longer have the luxury of multiple tabs open at once, all the time.

TIME MANAGEMENT

- You may have found a rhythm while WFH where you devoted a certain chunk of time to calls/meetings, allowing you to devote a separate chunk of your workday to "heads-down" or "deep work" (in other words, work without interruptions). Find a way or space to do this when returning to the office. When you're in person, it is easy for people to ignore the fact that you might be in the midst of "deep work" and come by your desk to strike up a conversation. If necessary, hide in a conference room to recreate a quiet space similar to what your bedroom or home office may have provided.

- If your company allows you the luxury, schedule your WFO and WFH days around your personal life (or vice versa). If you know you have a doctor's appointment near your apartment on Wednesday, perhaps that is a better day to WFH. If you know you have a long line of meetings with important stakeholders on Friday, perhaps that is a good day to go into the office so you don't risk your roommate surprising you with their loud music while you try to focus on an important call.

Taking time to evaluate what practices serve as the *best of both*, and proactively changing your behavior in each setting, will ensure you're kicking ass no matter the location of you or your colleagues.

6.
BENEFITS: WTF

If you are blessed with the ability to stay on your parents' health insurance for years to come, by all means, do so. If you are in the opposite predicament and have to sign yourself up for your company's benefits all by your lonesome, this chapter is for you. When I think of benefits that a company might offer its employees, I divide it into two parts: the Nitty-Gritty and the Fun Stuff. Your firm will have a designated benefits specialist that will help you walk through all of this when you first join. My biggest encouragement is to use that time with them wisely. Don't just let it flow in one ear and out the other, because you'll find yourself sending them frantic emails in a few months asking for help regardless.

THE NITTY-GRITTY

I consider all things medical, vision, and dental to be the Nitty-Gritty of benefits, with 401(k) coming in as runner-up. This is the aggressively boring stuff that no twentysomething wants to consider when looking into a full-time offer package, but trust me, it *is* important that you do. (If you don't believe me, skip to the chapter "It's All Fun and

Games Until You Tear Your ACL." We'll get more into the weeds of the possible run-ins you may have with health insurance there).

Your company will likely have a few different health insurance plans you can choose from, each of which will satisfy personal needs differently and cost a different monthly premium. I can't tell you which option will be the right one for you, but as someone who has opted in for both a high-deductible and a PPO plan during their short tenure I will give you a quick rundown of what I found to be the pros/cons of each.

HIGH-DEDUCTIBLE PLAN

Pros

- Typically the lowest cost plan.
- Employers often given a contribution to your HSA (Health Savings Account).

Cons

- You pay for everything out of pocket (or with your HSA) until you hit your deductible.
- Some of my prescriptions cost more under this plan than PPO.

PPO OR UNLIMITED PLAN

Pros

- Consistent co-pays for office visits.
- Seems that insurance covers more of the cost for other aspects of your visit than they do with the High-Deductible Plan.

Cons

- Costs more per paycheck for coverage.
- Depending on how often you go to the doctor, I'm not convinced it ends up saving you money in the long run compared to HDP.

Regardless of which plan you choose, my biggest and best parting line of advice for you is: *be prepared to spend more than you think you should every time you go to the doctor.* I still have not figured out the rationale behind what insurance does versus does not cover. Or why you still seem to spend so much money even when a provider/service is "in-network." I could go on for days.

Dental and vision benefits operate in a similar manner as health insurance in the sense that you can expect a monthly deduction to be taken from your check should you opt into coverage. Fortunately, I have worked for a company that completely covered dental and vision, therefore did not charge employees a monthly premium when it came to the annual basics (e.g., cleanings, eye appointments, etc.). Like health insurance, dental and vision benefits will vary from company to company.

401(K)

The 401(k) is a big one for me. Not only should you make for damn sure that you are putting money into one immediately after you start working full-time, but ask your firm whether or not they contribute matches! What is an employer 401(k) match? It's free money towards your retirement! For every dollar you put into your 401(k), you employer will match that contribution (up to a predetermined maximum percentage annually). It may not seem like a lot, but it begins to add up fast. You'll also want to ask if they have a vesting period for said match. Sometimes a company will require you to stay a certain length of time in order for you to be able to keep the money that they contributed to your account during your tenure. A standard company match is typically 2–4 percent of your annual salary. A good or competitive match is anything over 4 percent. Call me extra, but I have high expectations for 401(k) matches! If it's not 6 percent, I'm not interested.

THE FUN STUFF

Benefits I consider to be the Fun Stuff are the shiny perks that companies like to wave loud and proud to lure in new employees, especially of the latest generation. What the newest and coolest company perks are definitely change as time passes. For instance, I predict that flexible/remote working policies will be the next biggest thing now that the COVID pandemic is beginning to settle down and folks are slowly being called back into the office. Examples of hot new benefits that were once all the rage are Unlimited PTO Plans, Mental Health Sick Days, catered lunches, cool office snacks, and allowing employees to bring their pets to work.

Over time, what was once cool (remember scooters, nap rooms, and foosball tables?) and unique to a company becomes a baseline expectation across all firms. After working for a firm that catered lunches on Fridays and provided snacks for employees, I would probably give a recruiter a strange look if they said their firm did not provide similar offerings for their employees. As easy as it can be to get lost in the extras, it is most important to maintain a Nitty-Gritty mindset when evaluating benefits packages. Working for a company that puts more resources into the Fun Stuff than they do the Nitty-

Gritty might be a costly trade-off in the long run.

7.
TAKING PTO

As silly as it might sound, taking PTO (Paid Time Off, or sometimes referred to as "Vacation Days") is something I struggled deeply with as an entry-level employee. I always felt uncomfortable asking for time off. Even though I was allocated a fixed number of days I could take off annually, like every other member of the organization, I felt like I didn't deserve to since I was new. Do yourself a favor and believe me when I say *this is a ridiculous mindset to have*. And if anyone in your organization makes you feel otherwise, they are wrong.

Taking time off is not only your right (and frankly it's cool to be paid to have fun and have a life outside of work), but it's equally beneficial for the company. Human beings are not designed to run themselves into the ground working 365 straight days per year. If we were forced to, we would all reach a point of no return with burnout and what I like to refer to as mushed meat brain aka being so exhausted it's hard to string a cohesive thought together, much less succeed in delivering a big project. Embracing our weekends and a generous amount of PTO allows us the time that we need to *recharge* in order to be effective in our workweeks.

So, take your PTO. Take all of it. It's there for a reason, and even more so when you're young and fun and (relatively) responsibility-free. Your more senior colleagues will even benefit when you take PTO, because they'll get to live vicariously through your care-free vacations as they save their PTO for more mature adult things, like their child's school play or taking time off to work on their side hustle.

Keep in mind, there is a difference between "taking PTO" and "using PTO." Taking means you blocked your work calendar and took a vacation day, but *really using* it is a whole other ball game. To really use PTO, you must refuse to check your emails, sign out of your IM account, and go off the work grid. This is the only way you're going to recharge the way PTO is intended. Do this while you can, because eventually there will come a day in your career where you are trying to *really use* your PTO day, but can't, because your colleagues somehow all have your personal number and are ringing you with questions.

I look back at the first time I took a significant chunk of PTO a few months into my first full-time role and how glued I was to my email account with paranoia. I laugh at that naïve version of myself, wishing that Baby Brooke knew that only a short two years later she could light her cell on fire and throw it off a balcony and somehow she'd still be contacted by her colleagues asking for help during her time off. A dear friend of mine I worked closely with used to have a running joke of "I'm not [insert CEO's name here], so quit calling me." You aren't the CEO. You sure as shit aren't *paid* like the CEO. And I am sure your firm's CEO manages to turn their phone off on nights, weekends, and PTO days. So you should too!

8.
STRATEGIC ASS KICKING

Now that we've covered the very tactical basics, it's time to dive into higher-level strategies for starting off your first several days on a successful foot.

DOMINATING DAY ONE

Everyone's first day at work will look different. For those of you joining a large company you might participate in an extended onboarding program alongside the several other entry-level hires within your cohort. For those who are starting out at a smaller organization, your First Day Orientation might be presented to a much smaller group (you and up to a couple other employees of varying tenure and roles). It may even be presented to no one but you. The latter was the case for me. Whether your First Day Orientation experience is big or small, you can leverage the same prep work.

BE PHOTO-READY

Odds are you will be in front of a camera at some point during your first day. Whether it be a photo with your analyst cohort that will be posted on corporate social media channels or having a photo taken for your employee ID badge, be sure to brush your hair and select your outfit accordingly!

DON'T PACK A LUNCH

Someone, somewhere, will very likely want to take you out to lunch on your first day. Catered lunch might even be baked into the First Day Orientation program if it runs long enough. If the orientation does not run for a full day, your team and/or manager may very well have plans to go out as a group. If your manager or team aren't taking you out, you will likely have other new hires in need of a lunch buddy for the day. Regardless of where the wind takes you for your first day lunch, it's best to leave the lunchbox at home so you're a free agent. Walking with others to lunch is a great way to build relationships across the organization—which is especially important to kickstart on Day One.

BRING A NOTEBOOK

Take notes during your orientation. Even if you're not jotting down every word presented on the slide deck, you can list questions, make notes of things that might be good to look into further (such as benefits or your company intranet), or write down names/emails of people you should network with at a later date. Even if taking notes doesn't serve any other purpose than keeping your hands busy to help subside any first-day nerves, pen and paper is a handy thing to have with you should you need it.

QUESTIONS TO ASK YOUR MANAGER

I'm sure at some point during your First Day you will sit with your manager or another senior member of your team who will help delegate your work throughout your time in the group. Regardless of who you sit with, you can leverage this opportunity with a stack of starter questions.

CONFIRM YOUR TEAM'S CORE WORKING HOURS

This will look different for every organization and will even vary from team to team within the same firm. Clarify what your team's expectations are around daily start and end time, along with how strict they are regarding punctuality. Determining when you are expected to arrive to work, leave, take lunch (or skip if they allow it), how long lunch should typically be, and how flexible timing is for each phase of the workday should be done sooner than later.

INQUIRE ABOUT COMMUNICATION PREFERENCES

Is your manager a big email buff? Would they rather you just call them when you have a question? Do they prefer you pop into their office to chat in person? Do they prefer you just ping them over Slack, Teams, or another collaboration tool? What are the communication norms across your broader team?

You don't have to bombard them with each of the questions I've just listed. I did that to illustrate how many different approaches there are to staying in touch with your manager. Keep it simple by asking how they prefer to stay connected throughout the workday/workweek and your team's communication norms. Establishing preferences up front can help you avoid your messages getting glossed over and/or unintentionally annoying your manager by reaching out in a way that gets on their nerves.

For example, your manager might have an overly inundated email inbox, therefore preferring you call them directly if you have questions or need urgent feedback during the day. They might prefer you keep them cc'd on everything for visibility, or not at all to keep their inbox less cluttered. There are some nuances to communicating with your manager and/or team that can only be discovered with time, but asking them for baseline preferences early on benefits everyone in the long run.

IDENTIFY KEY PEOPLE TO ARRANGE INTRODUCTIONS WITH IN YOUR FIRST SEVERAL DAYS

It is not uncommon for people other than your manager to work closely with you or assign you projects. Your first few days will likely be a bit slower than usual, so it's a great time to reach out to stakeholders you will be working closely with or for. Ask your manager for a list of folks you can begin reaching out to, and ask those individuals the same thing when you meet with them. Before you know it, you'll be well-integrated into key groups before your project work takes full form.

GETTING ACCLIMATED TO YOUR ORGANIZATION

This somewhat piggybacks off of the networking bit we just discussed, but extends beyond reaching out to your key stakeholder groups individually. Introductions to other teams and 1:1 networking are just a small piece of getting yourself familiar with your new corporate home. Other key areas that are worth diving into during your first few weeks include researching your company's norms and policies, establishing your commuting routine, and personalizing your desk setup.

SURF THE INTRANET

Your firm likely has some form of intranet or shared drive that holds a plethora of data about your company, including personnel, how it operates, its culture, key objectives for the forthcoming year, etc. Ask someone on your team to point you in the direction of your firm's intranet and surf through it in your spare time during your first few days. This is especially important if you've landed a full-time role in an industry you're not very familiar with yet. For instance, my first full-time gig was in FinTech (financial technology). I had no prior domain knowledge about financial markets coming into this role. When scrolling through the intranet and our internal learning & development platform, I was very surprised at how many resources my firm made available to its employees so they could come up to speed with basic facts/terminology about financial markets. Absorbing this information during downtime my first few weeks helped me feel more confident during my 1:1 intro meetings with other employees and as I began working on projects.

TIPS FOR COMMUTERS

Most of us will be commuting to work in some way, shape, or form. Now, it should be noted that there are big differences in commuting either by foot or public transit in a big city such as NYC or Chicago and commuting via car in freeway-friendly cities like Los Angeles or in smaller cities with less functional public transportation options. But one huge similarity applies across both options: commuting sucks up a large chunk of your day. Here are some tricks to make the best of it.

BUY A BIG ASS BAG

This might be more relevant for my public transit folks, but the same could be advised for those commuting by car. This big ass bag could be a backpack, a gym duffle, a tote, or a huge purse. Regardless of its shape, it should be big enough to hold spare clothes and shoes, a notebook, a water bottle, and on a good day a packed lunch. Also, it might not incur immediately, but soon enough the pressing business of your workday will ensure the only way you can still do things like working out or grabbing drinks with friends is if you do so right after leaving the office. Your desk will become a part-time closet, and you'll need a big ass bag on deck to carry whatever obscure items you might need to switch gears.

NO SHAME IN SNEAKS

Dress for comfort, not for speed during your commute—especially if you're walking or taking public transit. I used to want to look hot for every stranger I locked eyes with on my morning subway ride, and suffered through the pain that came along with standing in my heeled booties for forty-five minutes. This stubbornness and character building only lasted for about six months until I finally said fuck it. I bought neutral colored booties and flats (either tan or black) that would match just about any outfit I wore to work. These became my work shoes, and never left my desk drawer at the end of the day. I then bought a pair of commuter sneakers that would kindly escort me home at the end of the workday, and resurface again in the morning for the trek into the office once more.

MAKE A CVS RUN

You really don't realize how much time you spend at work until you start to work full time for a consistent period. Sure, we all know we're expected to work forty hours, but it doesn't really hit you how long forty hours is until you do it day in and day out. That said, set your desk up for success in every way imaginable. Just like you might invest in the work shoes that never leave the office, you may find it useful to do the same for toiletries. Take a trip to CVS (or another drug store) with your Big Ass Bag and buy floss, mouthwash, lotion, deodorant, ChapStick—whatever your hygienic heart desires—and keep it all at the office. Even if you don't routinely need these items, you might need them to freshen up for the after-work drinks you're bopping off to without the chance to stop at home first.

LOOK INTO DELIVERY SERVICES

Sticking with the same theme of "forty hours feels longer than forty hours sounds," you'll likely start to feel like there isn't enough time in the day to do everything you'd like. When I would commute into the office five days per week, I found it nearly impossible to also manage my time well enough to where I could work my forty-plus hour week while also making time to go to the gym daily, cook dinner, and prep my lunches. Things like laundry, grocery shopping, or other chores were just about impossible to squeeze in M–F.

Do yourself a favor and scope out all the obscure delivery services we now have at the tips of our fingers *before* you get really busy in your new commuter lifestyle. That way you can skip past the "overwhelmed with life" part of commuting and have Amazon. deliver your groceries directly to your door from Day One!

PART TWO

EVERYTHING ELSE

9.
THE FIRST FUCK UP

I wish I told you after the first fuckup, there were seldom more that followed.

Lol. Wrong.

The inevitable part of working full time within a business is fucking things up. Some are little baby fuckups, like accidentally misspelling the CEO's name in a company-wide email (while incredibly embarrassing, it will soon be forgotten). Some are big ol' scary fuckups that will keep you up at night, or wake you from your slumber if you actually manage to fall asleep. You may think I'm being dramatic, but this is the real life of a twentysomething trying to keep their head afloat in the corporate world.

Autonomy is both a blessing and a curse. I find myself running on the same hamster wheel of *WTF are they giving me so much responsibility for; I hate having so much autonomy—I am so new to working, this is stressful,* coupled with the complete opposite perspective of *Hell yeah, I am doing my thing, speaking up in meetings, putting together proposals, having ideas that people agree with; I am making money moves with this autonomy—don't take it away!*

When things go well, I tend to think and embody the latter. When I fuck things up, I tend to retreat to the first. Until one day, about three months in, I finally told myself to grow up. Why was I complaining at all about something (autonomy) that has only recently been normalized for employees at all levels of an organization? From listening to my coworkers who have been in the corporate world much longer, it seems that autonomy, respect, and responsibility were not a minimum requirement of employers even ten years ago. People accepted the shit they were served by management and smiled about it, because they had to.

Presently, we live in a "candidate's market" and have the luxury of demanding more of our employers. Some candidates more than others, depending on the skills they possess. We want flex work, aggressive growth trajectories, large amounts of trust and autonomy, meaningful project work . . . the list goes on. Regardless of the fact that nowadays these offerings are the bare minimum employees expect from nearly all employers, do not take them for granted!

Nonetheless, when I would screw things up (from small things like forgetting to inform a candidate of their scheduled interview time, to bigger things like somehow shattering the company's iPad screen during my career fair travels), I found myself getting flush-faced, irritated, and blaming autonomy.

Well this is what they get for expecting so much out of me.

Why did nobody buy cases for these fucking iPads?

So . . . how can I spin this so I am not shirking responsibility but it also doesn't look like my mistake?

Cut it out. The sooner you dig deep and find the ability to say "I messed up," the better off you and your broader team will be. Not the kind of "I messed up" that is said under your breath, or only when you are forced to explicitly admit it. Nor the "This was my mistake, I will improve next time" that you tell everyone else *except for* your direct manager who is responsible for your feedback and performance reviews. I am talking about the big ol' scary, ugly, *extremely* difficult, proactive, complete and total ownership of your actions—partnered with confidence in yourself that you were well-intended and did not mean for negligence or misjudgment to win this round.

Everyone at every level of an organization makes mistakes of varying degrees of "bad." If there is one thing you are not alone in (as you *will* feel alone in many ways your first full-time year), it is this.

I get it. Just knowing that everyone fucks up here or there won't diminish the humiliation you will likely feel following the first several fuckups you experience yourself. Beyond talking yourself off a ledge, reassuring yourself that everyone fumbles, and reframing how you think about making mistakes (less *I fucked up bad* and more *I recognize I have a gap here, and this is a learning moment*), I don't have much advice for how to change how you *feel* when you do fuck up. Because feeling a bit uncomfortable, disappointed, or embarrassed when you make a mistake is inevitable. However, I do have some tips for how to avoid the uncomfortable nature of fucking up in the first place.

STARTING SMALL

How do you ensure you'll ace a test? You study. How do you learn your lines for the lead role in the spring musical? You rehearse over and over. How do you run a half marathon? You stick to a training plan that begins with a single mile and build your way up to 13.1. The same idea applies for getting more comfortable messing up at work—it's all accomplished through repetition and practice.

Let me clarify; I don't mean practice messing up, as in deliberately make mistakes in order to acclimate yourself for when you mess up organically. I mean practice *owning your mistakes and mess-ups*. Practice makes perfect and the perfect way to start owning your fumbles is to begin doing so with the smallest of mishaps and work up your courage from there. I have had an incredible and disproportionate amount of anxiety for blips as insignificant as misspelling someone's name in an email greeting. Sure, it's eye-roll worthy when someone sends an email asking me to do something for them and they address me as *"Broke"* instead of *"Brooke."* But an oversight like that will be forgotten in an hour's time. Yet I would (literally) lose sleep over it when I hit send faster than I could catch a spelling error. If I was that anxious about the small blips, imagine how I reacted when I actually fucked up to a more memorable degree.

What helped me prepare for the uglier fuckups was being bolder about my smaller mistakes. I had to trust that my colleagues knew me well enough to know any oversights I made—from spelling errors and typos to forgetting to dismiss key candidates from the interview cycle in an appropriate window of time—were not intentional (nor was I an idiot). If anything, the little blips were a by-product of running at 100 mph all day every day. Being bold and owning my small errors as they came brought a sense of confidence and security I wasn't expecting when I initially began this exercise. Getting comfortable with the fact that small errors couldn't be avoided and normalizing imperfection gave me some breathing room.

Practicing some of the below phrases over and over slowly desensitized me from the sting of admitting I was wrong, and resulted in a significant decrease in anxiety over things I really shouldn't have been sweating in the first place.

- "Unfortunately urgent items have come up and I won't

have time to complete your ask by end of week. I will
have this back to you as soon as possible."

- "I wasn't able to get a hold of all of the stakeholders I
  needed to in order to complete your ask."
- "I misunderstood."
- "I leveraged the wrong data. Please use this updated
  version."
- "I didn't realize we were ready to propel this forward. I'll
  send it out now."
- "That one is on me. I misread your instructions."
- "I take ownership for that. How should I better approach
  this scenario next time?"
- "I should have asked for help and will be sure to do so in
  the future."

Notice none of these phrases use the word "sorry." I wrote them
that way intentionally. We aren't practicing saying "sorry" because
these things happen. Sorry implies guilt, and we're not feeling guilty
for making an honest oversight. Saying sorry when it isn't warranted
not only dilutes your apologies when they need to matter, but it also
gives away your power. We can be sorry for any of the adverse effects
that occur because of our blips, sure. But we are not obligated to be
sorry for the blips themselves.

Sorry = guilt = anxiety = no good.

Finding a little bit of grounding and security in the inevitable flubs
that come with working will make thinking through and rectifying
notable mistakes much easier. It will allow you to think through
solutions with a clearer mind, rather than being totally consumed by
embarrassment and too flustered to act quickly.

ASK FOR HELP BEFORE YOU GET THERE

Put your ego aside and ask for help. Did you find yourself getting slightly offended after reading that? Don't be! Having an ego isn't a bad thing. However, evading the fact that you do have an ego is. Egos are like feet; everyone has 'em and they all stink. I recommend we all put our egos aside to ask for help in the face of uncertainty, as it's much easier to ask for help in order to *prevent* a fuckup than it is asking for help *fixing* one after the damage is done.

Collaboration is an absolutely beautiful thing, and if you find yourself part of an organization that genuinely celebrates and encourages collaboration, you are extremely lucky. I learned so much and saved myself from so many potential fuckups by working in an extremely collaborative team in my first role as a junior recruiter. There was no email too small for me to peek over and ask my beloved colleagues, "Can you give this a quick proofread before I click send?" and vice versa. They frequently asked me—*less than a year experience working full-time, me*—to proofread their content too. Much to my surprise, sometimes I even added value! It feels good not only to help others polish and perfect their output, but having someone return the favor for your work. Knowing someone has glanced over your work before submitting it gives you an extra shred of confidence that your output is of quality and will be well received.

Try to identify who on your team might be able/willing to fill this kind of "editor in chief" role for you and your projects. If you perform a few different key functions in your role, you may go to different people to review different things. For instance, in my current role, I always lean on the data science team leads for spot-checking business management–related tasks before I send any presentations or data visualizations upstream to leadership. Often they just give a thumbs up that my first draft is good enough to share, but other times they'll catch a silly mistake or think of adding content that I didn't initially consider. When it comes to project management–related items I am preparing for the data science leads, I may lean more closely on some of the other PMs I work with cross-functionally for feedback. For quick sanity checks or asking dumb questions without judgment, I have a short list of people on deck, some of whom have volunteered for this position, and most of whom I appointed myself (ha ha).

If you do pick up the habit of having someone review the majority of your work prior to submitting it, you might find yourself in a predicament of spot-checking versus timeliness. When you loop in someone else to help look over your tasks, you must be mindful of their competing tasks and availability. Sometimes you just don't have time to build in a day or so buffer in the event someone is very consumed by their own deadlines. If you find yourself here, depending on the task, you may want to defer your own delivery date for the sake of having a thoroughly reviewed output. You'll want to do some quick analysis on the urgency of the task vs. uncertainty in your output.

If it's a very low-urgency task (i.e., no firm due date—a "finish as you can" project) with high uncertainty in your output (i.e., you're not confident you calculated everything correctly), you probably want to wait until your trusty editor can provide some input.

On the contrary, if it is a high urgency task (e.g., response to an email you should've sent days ago) with low uncertainty in your output (i.e., small chance you'll fuck up your response), you're probably safe to just go for it.

For example, delaying the deployment of an internal, team-wide survey by a few hours so someone has time to review your grammar and continuity is well worth the wait. You might *hate* having to miss a deadline you set yourself, but the benefits of being thorough and providing a seamless survey experience for the team members strongly outweighs sending a half-assed survey that might confuse people just for the sake of being on time. I promise the world will keep spinning if you have to defer less significant deadlines to ensure accuracy. If you're concerned that is not the case, ask your manager for guidance.

SERVE YOUR FUCK UP WITH A SIDE OF SOLUTION

I know you are going to die trying to avoid fucking up. I wish we lived in a world where we never had to cross that bridge, but unfortunately we do not. So not if, but *when*, you find yourself riding an "*oh fuck*" moment, I always recommend proposing a few solutions alongside your mistake when updating your manager or peers on what occurred. Doing this has two primary benefits:

1. It softens the blow a bit.
2. It shows that you are committed to quickly fixing the issue that you've created.

My thought process is if giving candy to a baby works to distract them from the fact that you're taking away the earring they shouldn't be chewing on in the first place, the same method can work for taking away positive outcomes from your employer. Naturally, this is more difficult to pull off in real time (e.g., realizing during the middle of a meeting that you've made a blunder). If you manage to think on your feet and throw out a few sound approaches for rectifying what has occurred, that's amazing and you should get a gold star for the quick thinking. It can never hurt to come overly prepared and appear overly thoughtful when bringing up issues or observations to your boss or peers, so you should absolutely think through a few ways in which you can overcome the mistake that has been made.

My first notable fuckup had to do with budgets for our forthcoming internship class. Money is definitely not something you want to screw up, but alas, I managed to find a way to do it. The fact that I made a mistake involving numbers was especially painful for me to experience because of my deep-rooted self-consciousness regarding my math and technical abilities. It was also a ding to my pride because I like to think of myself as extremely diligent and detail-oriented. Yet here I was, fat fingering an Excel spreadsheet that resulted in an over-allocation of summer housing stipends for our intern class.

The way our internship program operated when I oversaw the recruiting process was we awarded a limited number of stipends to cover housing expenses for out-of-state students. We gave these out on a first-come-first-serve basis. The limited number we had within budget typically got us through the entire recruitment cycle without issue, since many applicants would end up being local to the Greater NYC Area. Someway, somehow, I miscounted how many stipends we had left to extend and mistakenly allocated one over what our budget allowed. Thankfully these weren't million-dollar stipends, so it's not like I put the company at risk of going under with my mistake. But still, it was a decent chunk of money and whether it was ten dollars or ten thousand dollars I would still be embarrassed that I made such an avoidable mistake. Stricken with panic, I started thinking through how we could detract in other areas to ensure that the awarded stipends remained, despite going over budget.

* * *

I started incorporating the above mantras in my day-to-day after the first time I witnessed someone properly own a mistake. Early on in my tenure, a colleague I deeply respected calmly and confidently owned a small blip (similar in magnitude to what we discussed in the "Starting

Small" section). They did so without hesitation and without even the slightest attempt to pass the blame off to another individual. They owned the small oversight, didn't apologize for it because they didn't need to, and moved on with grace and poise. It was unlike anything I had ever done myself when coloring a bit outside of the lines.

This observation might have been so insignificant in nature to some; my colleague probably never thought twice about the interaction or the blip because it truly wasn't a big deal. Regardless, it resonated extremely strongly with me. I had never had the courage to stand in my mess. Big or small, notable or unmemorable, I have always squirmed when I mess up. And if I've ever owned up to it on the front end, I've done so only when I absolutely had to. To see someone own it the way they did, unfazed by the event and confident in their attempt, was so eye-opening, and helped me realize what a poor job I was doing myself when accepting ownership of my mistakes.

My difficulty in admitting fault is really rooted in the fact that I have crippling guilt when I let people down, but that doesn't matter. Despite the reason *why* it's difficult to own up to your mistakes, it's not a very respectable quality.

That said, start now. Practice the steps provided above sooner than later. Put your hands on your hips, puff out your chest, tip your chin up in "power pose" fashion, look in the mirror and say, "I, [insert full name here], completely and royally fucked this up." And believe yourself. Believe you were wrong, but also believe that being wrong is completely OK.

Owning your actions is uncomfortable and embarrassing because of the underlying assumption that as brand-new professionals we will be perfect or as close to it as we can get. It is anxiety-inducing because of the underlying assumption that mistakes are bad, and the misguided notion that people will think we are the mistakes that we make.

Let's normalize messing up. Let's practice saying it each time we do it to desensitize ourselves from the sting associated with flubs. Let's find peace in the fact that we will absolutely not be perfect at any point in time. Furthermore, we should understand that what is deemed as "perfect" will vary from manager to manager, team to team, company to company—which makes achieving perfection out of anyone's reach (because like many things in our world, perfection is a construct).

Be comfortable in your skin, confident in your critical thinking skills, and believe that people will see you are well-intended. Come to terms with the fact that you will make messes as you learn and grow; and do so sooner than later, for your own success and sanity.

10.
GET A HOBBY, HUNNY

I want to start this chapter off by making clear I did not stumble upon this piece of advice by myself. One of my dearest and most cherished colleagues said this to me way early on, and after giving it some thought, not following through because I'm a lazy idiot, and then *finally* acting on it over a year later —I am here to validate this piece of advice and encourage you to skip the "lazy idiot" part and act on this ASAP.

Get a hobby.

And no, Bottomless Brunch Saturdays do not count. I mean a *real* hobby that can act as an obligation beyond work and serve as a portion of your identity. This is important for any young professional to establish early on in their career and prioritize accordingly because it helps establish boundaries and provides another area of life to look forward to and/or judge your performance. Both of which are incredibly important for your mental health and overall well-being.

The colleague who gave me this gem of advice did so while we were discussing how the stress of work had slowly consumed every aspect of my life and I was finding it very difficult to "switch off" either at night before going to sleep or even while out with friends on the weekend. She validated me in my struggles and said something along the lines of:

"Look, Brooke. I go home to a family that I have to care for, so I have no other option but to switch off. I have other obligations that require my attention. Young professionals may not necessarily have that. It might be good for you to find a hobby that requires the same amount of attention. It will force you to switch off from work and also make the weight of what happens here feel less heavy."

It blew my mind. I had felt the effects of not having hobbies to help me decompress/distance myself from work, but was unable to trace these feelings back to the source. Until my colleague shared this little gem of wisdom, I did not realize how much of a negative effect not having other activities to look forward to, prepare for, and commute to was having on my life. After recognizing that the majority my feelings of unfulfillment and burnout were coming from the lack of hobbies in my life, it made perfect sense to me.

I had just left a collegiate lifestyle of death by student involvement. I was so involved in the most random ass assortment of clubs and organizations, to the extent that there were many days out of the week I had to bring several different changes of clothes with me to campus and run out to my car to change midday. My college experience was twelve hours daily of switching from sweats in class, to a blazer for student government meetings, to workout tights for the Zumba fitness classes I taught, to dresses for sorority functions in the evenings. Needless to say, upon graduating and starting a full-time job, I went from 100 back down to 0 in terms of diversity of activities throughout my day. It took me a while to even recognize how much this had affected my psyche.

Sure, I was still operating at "100" at work. I commuted nearly forty minutes each way from Brooklyn into the city to work nine-plus hours and squeeze in gym time immediately afterward, which made for an average of about twelve hours away from my apartment and bed, daily. Besides the gym, all of that time was spent going to and from the same place: my office. The monotony of a commuter lifestyle in a big city was new to me and very draining for an extreme social butterfly like me who was used to hopping and bopping all over my college campus.

For those who can't relate to excessive student involvement and designed their college experience to have little to no extracurricular commitment, you may still be able to relate to the underlying feeling I am describing. Because even if you didn't spend the past four years or so bouncing from student activity to student activity, you likely set aside long timeframes for sports and exercise, partying, schoolwork, reading, video games with friends, or midday naps to break up your day. All of which there is little to no time for once you begin working full time.

HOW HOBBIES HELP YOUNG PROFRESHIONALS

So what do hobbies do to solve the feelings of monotony, burnout, and even despair (dramatic, I know) that come with entry-level employees' adjustment to five days of their weeks now revolving solely around work? Believe it or not, they can do a lot beyond just simply breaking up your day or giving you something to look forward to.

BREAKING UP YOUR WORKDAY

I used to pride myself on how spontaneous of a human being I was. Living out the P in ENFP to the fullest extent, I seldom planned my weekend activities in advance and even more seldom said no when a friend asked if I wanted to join them on an adventure. The beautiful world of spontaneity seemed to drift away after I'd moved to New York and began working full time. It took many months for me to realize that I had experienced a pendulum shift from the "yes man of all yes men" to someone who refused to go to dinner with friends on a Sunday because it was a "work night." How did I make this dramatic shift in a matter of months?

It's because we so easily fall victim to routine after we begin working a nine to five, especially in a place like New York City, where your nine-to-five job is actually a seven-to-six (and sometimes *weekends*) job and the commute to work can easily eat up another 1–2 hours total of your day. Routine and structure kick in as a sort of survival instinct. You plan out every ounce of your weekday and weekend, otherwise there is no possible way you'll squeeze it all in. For someone who was adamant about consistently packing their lunch, working out, commuting to/from the office, and finishing everything on their work to-do list before heading home for the day, planning and structure was the only way I managed to accomplish it all. I went as far as "planning" to sleep only 5–6 hours per night to ensure I was able to get it all done.

I slowly began to catch myself saying no to midweek plans. I couldn't grab a drink with my colleague because I had to get home in time to meal prep lunches for the remainder of the week. I couldn't stay out any later than 8 p.m. to ensure I was home in time to get settled and get to bed so I could make the 5:30 a.m. workout class. In other words, I morphed into the person I swore I would never be, saying no to drinks and fun just so I could adhere to a strict schedule.

It was an easy pattern for me to fall into because outings with friends registered as "optional" in my brain. Now, had my obligations been something that seemed more mandatory, like weekly practice for an intramural Frisbee league, I would have had a more legitimate reason to put my to-do list down and leave work sooner. Or a better excuse behind why I didn't have time to meal prep and needed to buy lunch tomorrow. Had I found a hobby earlier, I would've reaped the benefits of breaking up the monotony of my workdays much, much sooner.

I'm sure part of you may be thinking, *Why can't my weekly Girls' Night Out break up my work week? Why does it have to be a hobby?* The answer is weekly GNO among other social activities absolutely can still break things up for you, but more times than not it might only give you so much space from work. Take it from someone who has had their fair share of midweek drunken dinners with the gals; these outings often break up your day physically but not mentally. How many times do you find yourself falling into the trap of talking about work, bitching about people at work, and the like when hanging out with friends? It's what friends are there for. While it's cathartic in the moment, you might leave your GNO feeling as if you never fully left the office, because part of your mind was still clearly there based off your topics of conversation at dinner. This limits the effectiveness of your "recharging dinner with the gals."

Conversely, if you had spent that time in a fitness class, at community theatre rehearsal, practice with your intramural Frisbee team, cooking lessons, book club, or your three-month UX/UI course, you'd be forced to totally and completely disconnect from your day-to-day during that period of time. In these types of activities you're surrounded by fresh faces, with varying passions and occupations, and therefore likely to strike up conversations about totally different things than you normally would with your crew of best friends. Having an activity to attend at least once per week as a sort of "home base" gives you the opportunity to totally step away from the corporate jabber that inevitably begins to seep into every aspect of your life.

ESTABLISHING BOUNDARIES

It's very easy to throw yourself into work and justify staying late, coming in early, or logging in on the weekends because you're a "young, single professional." Which is true, and can be a nice way to get ahead in your career. But like anything in life, balance is important. And just as true as it is that you can pour into work while you're young, single, and obligation-free, it is equally as true that you can pour into life while you're young, single, and obligation-free. Your side hobbies like photography, million-dollar business ideas, community theatre, skateboarding at your local park, running groups, etc., are all things that will naturally shift to the back burner of life if you end up in a high position that requires more attention in your career, have a family, have a significant other, or a family member you must care for, etc. So finding the time to invest in yourself while you are young is important.

Identifying what hobbies you'd like to commit to at least once per week will help force you into drawing boundaries for yourself. This is an especially good strategy if you find it difficult to say no and honor boundaries you set by and for yourself. Saying no is difficult when you are trying to impress your new colleagues; but I guarantee it becomes infinitely more difficult to do once you've established a track record of never saying no. This is why leveraging hobbies to establish boundaries between your work-life and personal-life best serves you when done sooner vs. later.

YOUR IDENTITY AND SELF-WORTH

I briefly mentioned this in the very beginning of the chapter, but it's worth hitting home on. Having another activity that you can tie your identify and self-worth to beyond work is probably the least obvious yet most critical benefit that hobbies can bring.

We've already made it clear in the previous chapter that fuckups can and will happen. Part of why young Profreshionals may be so hard on themselves when they make mistakes or fail to hit the major goals/ deadlines at work is because disproportionate amounts of value are placed on the "work" portion of their identify. Young Profreshionals are excited to join the workforce and are eager to kick ass in their new job. When a disproportionate amount of emphasis is placed on an aspect of one's identity, their actions in that realm of life hold a lot of weight. When something jeopardizes how one perceives their performance to be in that area, they are more likely to take it to heart.

For instance, if someone values being a parent above all else, and something happens for them to feel as if they've failed to be a good mom or dad, they'll take it harshly. For someone who values their relationship above all else, if they are perceived as a bad boyfriend or girlfriend it will be extremely difficult for them to get over. The same applies when someone values their work above all else. If they tank an important presentation, miss a huge deadline, or are passed up for the big promotion, it'll hit hard. It'll be difficult to swallow and even more difficult to recover from.

Having hobbies we deeply value helps us balance out how much emphasis and importance we place on our performance as an employee. If we are passed up for the big promotion but have the lead role in our community theatre show, it will still suck majorly, but at least we will have another activity to pour our time and energy into. Having that lead role will allow us to feel some semblance of importance and talent in the moments when work doesn't give us that. If we do something extremely embarrassing at work, rushing off to rehearsal for the remainder of the evening forces us to totally disconnect and stop fixating on what happened earlier that day.

A hobby isn't going to (and probably shouldn't) completely substitute how much you value work. It's just going to take the edge off a bit by helping you more evenly distribute how much you allow work to impact your overall perception of yourself. It's no different than if we only applied for one college and received one rejection letter versus applying to twelve colleges and receiving one rejection letter. It's always going to suck knowing you weren't good enough to land an acceptance at that one university, but having eleven additional acceptances may take your mind off of it. Your self-worth is likely to take a harder hit in the scenario where you applied for one and missed one, versus the scenario where you missed one but had eleven more to fall back on.

* * *

As a Profreshional, there is no doubt that you will place a heavy emphasis on your career. It makes sense for you to do so, considering starting full-time employment has been the biggest "new chapter" you have walked into in a few years' time. And many might say it's the biggest chapter you'll walk into for many years to come. That's a lot of pressure and excitement bundled into a single aspect of your life; there's no argument there.

Knowing that this "new chapter" will hold a lot of weight to you, it's important for you to get a head start on finding ways to balance it out. The sooner you explore your options and commit to exciting hobbies and side gigs, the less likely it will be that you find yourself in a situation where you really wish your list of priorities included things far beyond just kicking ass at work.

11.
BECOME THE EXPERT THEY NEVER KNEW THEY NEEDED

One of the greatest advantages to being new to an organization (or the working world in general, for that matter) is the doe-eyed naivety you carry with you during your first few months of employment. You're entering the corporate world completely unfamiliar with your company's existing social norms, archaic processes, toxic politics, you name it. While this may be daunting, I believe to my core it is what allows Profreshionals to yield the highest impacts in their first role.

I endorse the following three steps as the fast-track way to go from the newbie on the block to a key player on your team:

1. Look for gaps or inefficiencies.
2. Evaluate how to close these gaps and tighten any inefficiencies.
3. Be like Nike and Just Do It.

Boom. Simple. Before you know it, you're not only the *only* person on the team who gave a shit enough in the first place to notice an area of improvement to your department or organization's archaic processes, but you also took the initiative to implement the solution. You are now the SME (subject matter expert) of said process improvement and people will be looking to you to continue the legacy that is your new, super-cool-efficient-way of doing things.

BE LIKE NIKE AND JUST DO IT

Pay attention to how things operate around you. I mean really pay attention. Listen, absorb, take notes. Really give a shit. If it seems like your team consistently talks about a recurring issue, think of ways that pain point could be resolved. Ask questions about how current processes work, and clarify four times over if you have to. Once you feel confident that you have a good grasp on the existing gaps or pain points of your team, department politics, the approval process for various documentation, how to collaborate on new and recurring projects, etc., dig deep into your previous experiences and ask yourself, How can I make this better?

The opportunities for improvement you identify can vary in the amount of work required to enact change and the impact it has on your team/organization. I don't mean for you to put massive amounts of pressure on yourself to come up with the next best innovation of the decade for your firm. The types of improvements you make can be small and still yield great benefits.

For example, let's say a new hire named Jan works within a team that is dispersed across multiple time zones. Jan's team has always struggled to maintain a consistent level of collaboration and communication due to geographic location, but she has noticed the team is struggling even more than usual since everyone began working remotely during the Coronavirus pandemic. During her weekly 1:1 with her manager, Jan mentions her observation and proposes that she implement a few new meeting series to increase transparency across the team's workloads.

She suggests they initiate an optional, bi-weekly social hour where a team member selects an article for the group to read ahead of the session and they spend the meeting time discussing their thoughts on the piece. Concurrently, they can start a monthly staff meeting series where the team leads can discuss progress and/or setbacks of key projects and individual contributors can ask any questions they might have (about projects or the firm at large).

Jan's manager agrees that the team's communication and collaboration have suffered more than usual lately and is impressed that Jan took the initiative to propose a solution to the issue. Her manager is pleased for her to run with her ideas and lead both meeting series moving forward. These meetings not only positively impact the team's productivity, but put Jan in a great light with her manager and peers for being the one to tighten an existing gap.

Now that Jan leads both of these meeting series, she slowly begins to be nominated by her manager and peers to establish other efforts that relate to collaboration and team-building. Over time, she becomes the natural fit when her team needs someone to lead a learning and development initiative. She ends up doing such an exemplary job for her team that leaders of other departments ask her for advice on how to get similar efforts off the ground for their teams.

This is one very simple example of how you can identify a gap, propose a solution, implement it, and eventually become your team's local expert in a certain area. As long as you continue to be curious, are actively invested in how your team organizes/gets work done, and how effective the existing processes are, you too will find yourself having a Jan moment.

Like anything, the list of gaps or inefficiencies that will unveil themselves to you will be unique to your organization, team, and role.

However, to help kick-start your mission to *Be the Expert They Never Knew They Needed* I've proposed a few general problems areas new hires should keep an eye out for in hopes to recommend and implement a stellar solution:

- Improve collaboration (inter-team or cross-functional).
- Strengthen communication within your team or across different departments.
- Automation of processes using new tools or technologies.
- Establish frameworks for repetitive tasks.
- Improve standards for documentation.
- Eliminate redundancies and rework by aligning existing processes.

LONG-TERM BENEFITS OF EXPERTISE

As demonstrated in Jan's example, you can receive instant gratification from your manager or peers after implementing a solution for your team. However the glamour often does not stop there. The benefits of Becoming the Expert They Never Knew They Needed are twofold:

1. You make your life easier by improving the way your team gets work done.
2. Over time you become invaluable to your group.

The primary purpose of positioning yourself to be a SME (subject matter expert) extends well beyond receiving kudos from your manager. The entire point of being the go-to-guy-or-gal for the new solutions you propose is exactly how it's written: *You are now the go-to*. By recognizing areas in which your team or firm can improve and being the person to enact change, you have now strategically positioned yourself as the expert of the new process, structure, or tool that you've implemented. That likely means that from the moment the solution is implemented, you are now the person who will monitor its progress and effectiveness, and you will communicate the solution's ROI to middle management or leadership. You will be the person your team naturally begins to nominate to lead any iterative improvements or extensions to the solution that need to be made later on. You become the point of contact for all of your colleagues that need to be trained on the tool or process. You are the person that team leaders of other departments contact to ask about implementing a similar solution for their team.

Before you know it, you've evolved from an entry-level individual contributor to a subject matter expert for your team. Being one of the only employees to understand the intricacies of how any process or tool functions is an invaluable position to be in. Becoming the Expert They Never Knew They Needed doesn't guarantee your immunity from harm's way, because in reality everyone in any organization is dispensable, but it might get you as damn near close to it as possible.

* * *

As the new blood in our organizations, we are at the prime time in our career to ask questions and throw out new ideas—whether they turn out to be stupid, brilliant, or anything in between. This behavior is expected and encouraged from new employees, and failure is much easier to shake off and reframe as "learning moments" the earlier you are in your full-time tenure. The more time and experience you have under your belt and the higher in an organization you go, the less breathing room you may have to fumble. When you're just starting out, fumbling is expected, so you may as well lean into it.

Hiring managers and team members realize that most of the tactical functions of an entry-level role can be taught, and will be absorbed by the new hire over time. People don't expect you to be perfect as a new employee, but they do expect you to try. They expect you to show initiative, to demonstrate an eagerness to learn, to show that you are able to think critically for yourself. Finding gaps in processes and recommending solutions, taking ownership of implementing improvements to the way things run, helping a colleague with something they have on their plate and just do not have the bandwidth to complete, etc. are all excellent ways to demonstrate your capabilities early on. How impressed your teammates are with you as a new hire directly correlates with how much effort they see you putting in (with your initiative yielding awesome results being an added bonus).

So thinking back to the three core steps to Becoming the Expert They Never Knew They Needed, one of the easiest ways to stumble upon issues that need fixing is to ask a ton of questions early on in your career. When you ask your colleagues "Why do we do this thing that way?" and the response you receive is some variation of a) "Oh, well we always have," b) "I'm not sure, honestly," or c) "I haven't had time to explore alternatives," that is a key indicator that there is room to enact positive change to an existing process or habit.

If you are lucky enough to come across an opportunity like this in your first week, first six months, or at all, seize it and change it! Do not let that voice in your head talk you out of doing otherwise. It's easy for us to be fearful or anxious to raise or voice and propose new ideas, especially in our first year of employment. I get why it seems so daunting. Everything feels so new. Everything holds so much weight and the mere thought of suggesting a solution that may have been considered by your team before, or may be perceived as stupid, is mortifying. But thinking back to this time six months to a year from now and realizing you missed a perfect opportunity to carve out a unique role for yourself will be equally, if not more, mortifying, I assure you.

12.
DRINKING ON THE CLOCK

As an extreme extrovert and employee of a company where there are seriously so many awesome people employed, I *love* drinking at work events. I mean, I love a good time anytime anywhere, but getting to cut loose with folks you don't see on the weekends, yet are some of the most prominent people in your life because you spend 40+ hours with them every week, can be a ton of fun.

If you're someone who disagrees and would rather eat your left arm than drink with colleagues, that is fine. We are all entitled to our own opinion and I can see how you would rather not extend the amount of time you spend in a work setting any further than you already do. However, don't hate on the people who *love* work functions (and love drinking at work functions) because their perspective makes sense too. Coworkers are like family after a while.

Now, I am sure different teams, departments, and organizations have different drinking norms. I encourage you to scope out said social norms prior to going hard with your best work buds. But if you're like me and have little self-control, you'll skip the "social norms" part and dive headfirst into going hard at your first after-hours work event:

letting your phone die, requiring your colleagues to put you in a cab home since you can't call an Uber, and having to beg your cab driver to pull over and not leave you as you vomit on the streets of Brooklyn in ten-degree weather after midnight. (Yes, that is a true story. I don't regret it, but also would not recommend it).

So, how does one heed my advice, avoid my mistakes, and *slowly* dip their toe into the professional drinking scene? The first step is to fully understand the different types of *on the clock* drinking scenarios one may be subjected to. From there, you can establish a tolerance threshold for your behavior based on situational context and your organization's norms.

IN-OFFICE HAPPY HOURS AND EVENTS

Because you are not only surrounded by colleagues, but also in your office building, this is the scenario in which you should probably exercise the most self-control when consuming alcohol. Now, this is just a generalization; some companies let the tequila shots rip during a casual mid-Thursday afternoon happy hour. If that's the case, and you want to partake to the fullest extent, go for it. But for the most part, it is likely your organization will not be going this hard during the standard weekly in-office drinks. You'll want to tread a bit more lightly than your typical keg stands and body shots.

For your first few in-office happy hours, I recommend finding a friend or member of your team to attend afternoon drinks with and matching their pace. You don't have to make it overly obvious and finish your very last sip of wine at the exact same time they do, but you can keep an eye on their refills as a benchmark. When selecting your undercover drinking buddy, it may be safer to err on the side of conservative, rather than intentionally selecting the well-known office party powerhouse. Once you scope out a few of these events and get a feel for how often and how much folks are drinking, you can switch up your undercover drinking buddy to whoever more closely aligns with your personal drinking preferences.

In sum, the mid-afternoon happy hour scene is likely going to be more low-key than other drinking scenarios, so it may be best to reserve your sloppiest self for after-hours events or off-site corporate parties. Wine and beer is more commonly served in the office than hard liquor, which in itself provides a layer of safety for your levels of consumption. These in-office happy hours are an ideal place to pregame, and I highly recommend you treat them as such! If you make plans for dinner or drinks with friends (or other colleagues) to follow up the in-office happy hour, it will not only give you a guideline for pacing yourself, but will allow you to keep the momentum going and set yourself up for an all-around fun evening.

AFTER-HOURS HAPPY HOUR

To use a musical metaphor, I like to think of after-hours happy hours as the "Explicit" version of the previous scenario, in-office happy hours. They're the same "song" for the most part, but if you listen closely, the lyrics will vary slightly. The in-office version is a much more filtered version, appropriate for all audiences, while the after-hours version delivers a full range of colorful language. After listening to both versions of the song you will be able to determine whether or not the "Explicit" version is too much to handle, and ultimately land on which version you prefer better.

The after-hours happy hour crowd is comprised of the hardcore partiers of the in-office happy hour crowd. They're definitely not a one-drink wonder; they are the kind of people who want to keep the momentum going once they have a drink or two. You can always count on this group to continue every in-office happy hour into a full-blown evening event at the bar next door to the office, or make a reservation at a nice rooftop bar to celebrate any of their colleagues' accomplishments.

The after-hours happy hour folk are as well-intended a group as they sound. They genuinely just like to have a good time. That doesn't mean, however, the urge to gossip about work-related topics will subside. Let me warn you of how difficult it is to avoid talking about work when surrounded by people from work—and the further along in inebriation the group gets, the more loose-lipped the crew will get. If you're brand new to an organization, being witness to this kind of dialogue (or worse, asked gossipy questions directly) can be extremely uncomfortable. I don't know about you, but I surely did not want to be caught in the winds of talking smack about employees who weren't even present to defend themselves. I didn't want to have to answer questions about who the hottest or bitchiest members of our leadership team were, how often so-and-so failed to do their job correctly, or anything of the like.

New to the organization, I did not want to get the reputation as a member of the after-hours happy hours "talk shit clique." I'm nearly three years in now to working full time and it doesn't feel any less awkward when these situations arise. It may be my background in human resources that makes me extremely uncomfortable in these situations because I have the lessons of discretion and fair treatment toward all burned into my head. But I am grateful for it because there is no need to digress all of our conversations into gossip.

It is key to know that heavy gossip is not only a possibility, but likely inevitable when a crowd of people who work for the same company are in a room together outside of the confines of the office building. This doesn't mean you *shouldn't* tag along for the after-hours fun, but just be mindful that you may be pulled into some conversations that you'd rather not participate in. Come prepared to these events and perhaps have a few one-liners in your back pocket that can help you escape the hot seat should you be asked "Don't you hate how so-and-so never does a good job with this weekly report" or anything of the sort. Worst-case scenario, you can always pop into the bathroom and hide it out for a bit when the conversations turn sour.

CORPORATE EVENTS AND PARTIES

Shit can, *and likely will,* hit the fan at corporate parties. Your colleagues probably passionately look forward to the annual corporate events your firm throws, and have a long list of stories from Holiday Parties Past to share with you. If folks offer up the anecdotes, it is in your best interest to listen, take notes, and devise a plan as to how you will avoid becoming one of the many stories in their arsenal.

From what I know of corporate parties, they're almost all open bar and they can keep our dear HR departments busy. I have heard stories of people punching others in the face, jobs lost, hookups, people getting so drunk they (literally) hit the ground on the dance floor. What I encourage you to take from this is that you'll likely not be the worst behaved, so let loose and have a good time – just not *too* good of a time.

NOT DRINKING AT ALL

While this chapter is primarily about drinking in a corporate setting and what to look out for whenever you do, it's important to highlight what might be so obvious that people fail to remember: you and your colleagues can attend these events without drinking at all. Sure, alcohol consumption might be the underlying epicenter of these types of corporate gatherings for *some* of your coworkers, but I assure you there are plenty of employees who do not look forward to the Holiday Party solely for the open bar (and therefore don't capitalize on it while they're there).

If for whatever reason you cannot drink or choose not to drink while attending these events, you will not be alone. Do not let the "happy" in "happy hour" deter you from showing up and connecting with fellow peers or clients. Whether you have a glass of wine or water in hand while networking shouldn't make any bit of a difference (and if people treat you otherwise, kindly tell them to fuck off).

If you are someone who loves making the most out of the free booze at corporate socials, be sure you don't make your colleagues who do not relate feel out of place. Even the slightest bit of seemingly harmless banter about them "being a prude" or "taking the night off" can create an extremely awkward situation for someone who might already be self-conscious about showing up to these events with the intent to stay sober.

* * *

I've tried to hit home throughout this chapter that drinking norms and scenarios will vary greatly from organization to organization. What is most important for you to do before diving into the professional drinking scene is to establish what your tolerance threshold is *for your own behavior and reputation* and listen to that voice above all else.

We are all adults. Adults are allowed to, and often like to, drink alcohol. Copious amounts, at that. It seems scary and counterintuitive to combine alcohol and work, because we are preached at throughout the course of our teenage development that drinking is bad. Partiers in college are assigned a negative connotation. As difficult and unnatural as it may be given our upbringing, it is important to change the way we think about alcohol consumption upon our arrival to "adulthood" and corporate life. Our age and context has changed, therefore so should the "bad" label that we may have previously assigned to drinking.

Drinking is one of the many bloodlines of business; many networking events occur and deals with clients are often closed over a plethora of cocktails. It's nothing to shy away from. If anything, it's a great scene to embrace and participate in, as it could result in some really incredible developments in your career. However, protecting yourself *always* comes first. Taking the time to observe how others in your company drink, determining the types of drinkers that your employee base is comprised of, and intentionally selecting which type of those drinkers you want to be, is going to be imperative for your successful participation in company-sponsored drinking events.

13.
OFFICE CREEPERS

It's sad that this chapter has to exist, but unfortunately our society isn't in a place yet where everyone feels safe going to work every day. I know this idea may be difficult to come to terms with, because throughout college and during internships the corporate world is made out to be this big enigma of polish and professional savvy. (I believe this notion is partly what causes so much confusion and anxiety for entry-level new hires). But the truth is, like you, your colleagues are everyday, normal people, regardless of their tenure and title. That means some of your colleagues may also be mothers, fathers, sons, daughters, avid runners, artists, musicians, former collegiate athletes, avid skiers, regular churchgoers, alcoholics, drug users, the list goes on. That also means, unfortunately for you and everyone else around, some of your colleagues may or may not be Office Creepers.

Take [insert nearly every TV crime show here] for example. How many episodes do the creeps in question end up being "normal" seeming people? It sucks but the reality is that creeps are everywhere, and in the words of Agent Rossi from *Criminal Minds*, "Psychopaths are attracted to a uniform." This notion extends to corporate employees in blazers.

I sincerely hope you are treated with the utmost respect and kindness in any work environment you find yourself in. I hope you can read this chapter and never ever have to relate to what I am about to say. But in the unfortunate event that you find yourself crossing paths with an Office Creeper, I want you to have stories to refer back to so that you may feel empowered to voice your needs/concerns and know you are not alone in this. We'll kick things off by discussing exactly what an Office Creeper is, detail a few examples, and wrap up with two theoretical Office Creeper encounters and advice as to how you may handle a similar scenario.

Office Creepers come in many shapes and sizes. They all look, act, communicate, and create uncomfortable situations differently. Some types of Creepers may not bother you whatsoever, whereas another may completely destroy any sense of joy or safety you may feel coming into the office. Above all else, it is important to keep in mind that individuals will react differently to Creepers based on their own personal experiences. One is completely entitled to their emotions in regard to creepers, no matter where they may fall on the spectrum.

For instance, those who have previously been involved in toxic relationships or experienced assault or harassment in the past may react very sensitively to an Office Creeper. Even if they react sensitively, it's equally as possible for the individual to choose to internalize this stress rather than formally raise concern with their HR Department. There is no right or wrong way for an individual to feel, react, and act to a Creeper. I repeat, there is *no right or wrong way* for someone to handle any encounter they have with an Office Creeper.

If you take anything away from this book, please let it be the understanding that individuals perceive things *based on their own experiences.* These perceptions manifest in many ways in the workplace. It is very likely you will not understand other people's perspectives, just as it is likely they will not understand yours. You should check your judgment at the door and approach people and situations in this realm with kindness and understanding. Now that we have the housekeeping out of the way, let's get back on topic.

TYPES OF OFFICE CREEPERS

As noted above, Creepers come in many shapes and sizes, and all create discomfort differently. That said there are many Creeper types I likely missed—so just because someone does not tick any of the boxes below does not mean you should be any less vigilant, or you should ignore the little hairs that stand up on the back of your neck (aka your Creep-dar going off). Definitely listen to those little hairs. The below Creeper archetypes are merely intended to give you a point of reference based on the types of Creeps I've paid witness to during my short corporate tenure.

TOO CLOSE FOR COMFORT

This archetype typically starts out as an acquaintance and, slowly over time, evolves into a creep. This may make identifying their creepy behaviors a bit difficult, because you'll be torn at the fact that they were once just friendly. This internal conflict might make it difficult to take action and put a stop to the creeping, as you may be confused and feel as if you're being overdramatic or overreacting. The Too Close for Comfort is the type of creeper that will constantly IM you, beyond what seems normal for the rapport you've established with them. They try to create inside jokes with you during random meetings, and if you play along, proceed to take them a *little* too far. If you give this archetype an inch for the sake of being polite, they will misconstrue your intent and proceed to go a mile.

CREEP 'EM WITH KINDNESS

Similar to the previous archetype, you may not recognize that this type of creeper is a creep right off the bat. They too will begin as an acquaintance and over time evolve into a bit more persistent presence in your life than you find comfortable. This archetype is known for showering you with gifts beyond what is common or appropriate for colleagues, insisting on 1:1 happy hours which they volunteer to pay for, and wishing you well on life events that you never directly told them about, etc. It will come across as endearing at first, until the creeper continues this behavior at an aggressive pace.

SERIAL NICKNAMER

This creeper calls you by anything other than your real name. This may include but is not limited to: darling, sweetheart, baby girl, some variation of hun or honey, no matter who may be around to hear it. These creepers may be able to easily get away with this because they're popular among your colleagues. Onlookers may justify their behavior because of that. They say, "Oh, they don't mean anything by it". *Right . . .*

HOLIDAY PARTY HO

This creeper uses company events as their hunting ground and alcohol as an excuse for their less-than-upstanding behavior. You will likely find them dressing up in costumes for attention, handing out candy or some other form of party favor that goes along with the theme. Everybody in the firm recognizes they are a creep, yet somehow they're still employed.

CREEPERS IN ACTION

Seeing the Creeper archetypes written out may be enough to help you detect possible creepers in your workplace. But for the sake of being comprehensive, I want to go a step further and provide a few examples of theoretical encounters that unfortunately might unfold.

CREEP IN ACTION #1: CREEP 'EM WITH KINDNESS

Initially this colleague may come across as very friendly and supportive. They might frequently stop you in the café to chat about life, family, the basic coffee machine talk. No harm there, right?

Now, let's say one of your major hobbies is playing in a community band. Your first-ever performance with the group is in a few weeks and word gets out to your colleagues. This particular coworker mentions wanting to come see the show during your regular café chat, which is a very nice gesture. However as days pass, they continue to ask you to "text them the details"—a few times in person, a few times over instant messenger. Each time they ask, you try to deflect the request by sending them the link to purchase tickets directly. Another week passes and they stop you in the café area, asking why you "never shot them a text." After bringing it up several times, you begin to get uncomfortable. You aren't explicitly threatened by the individual, therefore maybe don't feel *unsafe* around them. But you are a bit creeped out from their insistence on you texting them. You might feel trapped; you do not want to damage a working relationship and/or appear like you are taking this series of events out of context. What do you do?

To figure out how to proceed, you could ask your manager (or someone else you trust) what to do. They might offer to handle it on your behalf, or empower you to tell your colleague you are happy to continue your rapport at work, but don't feel comfortable giving them your phone number.

CREEP IN ACTION #2: TOO CLOSE FOR COMFORT

This type of situation gets a bit stickier. Let's say you are an intern— bright-eyed and eager to attend all company "extras" in hopes to make a good enough impression to be extended a full-time offer at the conclusion of the summer program. A coworker frequently sits next to you during "lunch and learns," trying to make inside jokes, all seemingly harmless and friendly behavior that you are happy to go along with. Over time, they become very invested in the inside jokes you have, to the extent where they continuously send you unsolicited photos of things that relate to the jokes throughout the workday. This is where the red flags might begin to go off in your mind.

None of what this employee is doing is threatening in nature, but it is a bit . . . odd. As this progresses you become more uncomfortable, and feel more conflicted about saying something to your manager because you don't want to cause any trouble, especially as an intern. The Creeper then invites you to an after-hours happy hour across the street to send off a longtime employee who was leaving the firm. You learn that many people were invited to this event, but interns were not. Therefore you decide not to attend because you would feel out of place.

The weekend passes, and the Creeper stops you in the hallway Monday asking why you didn't attended the happy hour. They said they were looking for you throughout the night. You make up some lame excuse as to why you couldn't go, and they follow up with "Well, we don't need an event to get drinks together, how about we go out sometime this week."

Now you have a total WTF moment. This colleague not only didn't get the hint that you were beginning to get the creeps, but they would not let up. You start to become overwhelmed with stress, the creeps, and guilt that you "let this go on" for so long without saying something. You also feel an immense amount of pressure around the fact that you are an *intern*; you are new to the organization, and should you formally make a complaint, it would be against someone who has been at the company for several years. Where do you go from here?

Again, a safe next step is looking to your manager, another individual you trust, or HR for guidance. Whether you find the courage to tell this Creeper you feel uncomfortable and would like to cease contact, or prefer to let someone handle this difficult conversation on your behalf, there is no right or wrong.

YOU IN ACTION

If you are getting creepy vibes to *any degree* by someone in your workplace, you are absolutely within your rights to address it. You are also well within your rights to brush it off and not do anything at all. As we've touched on quite a bit, different folks will react differently depending on what degree of creep is being directed their way. Whether you plan to go out loud about the creepy encounters you've experienced, or choose to ignore them entirely, below are a few courses of action you may feel comfortable taking. Above all else, you should do what is going to make *you* feel safe and protected!

DOCUMENT CREEPY ENCOUNTERS

When I say "document" the encounters, I don't mean that you need to type forty pages single-spaced describing the details of the interaction.

You can absolutely do this if you want to, but even keeping a simple list of dates of when something creepy occurred in your iPhone Notes app will suffice. The point of documenting when encounters occur is to have a "case" that demonstrates the behavior has persisted over time. And it's ready in your back pocket should you ever decide you want or need to formally complain about the series of interactions.

TELL SOMEONE YOU TRUST

This is another way to document encounters. Inform someone who is a member of your organization, or tell someone like a family member or close friend who has no visibility into your company whatsoever. The benefit of telling someone as events occur is they can help you monitor your feelings as time progresses, and let you know if/when it seems your emotions are escalating. It can be hard to know if an emotion is intensifying, or whether or not a situation is "getting worse" when you're in it alone for so long.

Having a very trusted source watching things unfold from the outside can help you identify when things have gotten "worse" and it may be time to speak up. Even if things do not ever progress to that point, it is always beneficial to have someone to confide in, support you, and validate your concern. Having someone there to say, "You're right, they are a creep!" can go a long way for your sanity.

TELL YOUR MANAGER

Just because you want to speak up and ask for the creeping to stop does not mean you have to be the one to say it. Part of your manager's job is to defend, advocate for, and support you—not just in your professional day-to-day, but also in circumstances where you feel unsafe in the workplace. You should feel comfortable leaning on your manager to handle these conversations on your behalf, especially when the colleague performing the creeping is perhaps in a position of power, or might be someone you work closely with on your current team. I understand not all employees are graced with supportive managers, which is a shame. If you do not feel close enough to your manager to raise a concern of this nature, you are empowered to ask another mid-level manager you may feel better supported by, or your HR department.

TELL HR

Similar to your manager, your human resources department's job is to defend, advocate for, and support you—not just in your professional day-to-day, but *especially* in situations where you feel unsafe in the workplace. I know the HR skeptics of the world may make a rebuttal with "Wait, isn't the job of human resources to defend the company, rather than the employees?" They bring up a good point here. And no, they are not entirely wrong. But the way I encourage you to look at it is that employees *comprise* the company, and by protecting employees, especially in situations of harassment or "creeping," HR is protecting the company. Talking to someone you trust within human resources will help you knock out a few of these courses of action in one; HR will document the interaction, talk to the colleague performing the harassment, and hopefully the creeping will cease.

TELL THE CREEP TO BACK OFF

It's your creeper; you can tell them to back off if you want to. If you are getting tired of the persistent harassment and want to say something to the aggressor directly, by all means, you are empowered to do so.

If you want to have this conversation with the Creeper directly, you can do so in tandem with some of the other courses of action that we have already discussed. Typically if you bring a situation like this to your manager or HR, they will ask if you would like to have the conversation yourself or want someone else to handle it. For as many individuals that do not want to confront their harasser, there are just as many who do and would even prefer to. No one option is better than the other. Whichever route you choose, my messaging remains the same: Good for you for taking action to make your workplace a safer and more positive environment for yourself and others!

* * *

It is not my intention to dilute the gravity of these situations by writing them out in a concise and lighthearted manner. The scenarios within Creeper in Action read in a very linear manner, which might unintentionally discount all the internal turmoil and ambiguity that comes along with creepy situations. It is important to highlight that these situations are never as cut and dried as they might appear within text. They can be extremely confusing; relationships you build with your officemates might not always start out as creepy. Unfortunately they might start out as secure and evolve into something unsafe, either slowly or suddenly. When relationships take a turn like that it brings quite a bit of confusion and perhaps even guilt. The below thoughts might begin to consume your mind:

Did I do something to send a wrong message?

What if I am overreacting?

I never had the courage to tell them no or to stop, so I am at fault.

These thoughts, while maybe convincing, are wrong. They should not deter you from taking action if that is what you decide is best for you.

While this chapter uses humor to articulate a point about creepy interactions that can occur at work and possible ways to navigate them, there is *nothing funny at all* about workplace harassment of any kind. Whether it be sexual, racial, ageist, homophobic, related to ability/ disability, or otherwise, please know that harassment is not normal, not acceptable, not funny, and not something that you should ever feel you have to tolerate. My hope is that the archetypes and situations written above can be helpful to not only people who experience harassment directly, but employees who witness others being harassed. If you witness someone in your organization being on the receiving end of harassment, in addition to letting them know you are there to support them however you can, you can leverage the same courses of action to help them through their situation (being mindful they may want to handle it themselves first).

The scariest thing about seemingly harmless harassment is that it can very easily escalate to something much, much worse. For those who would like to read more on the impact that the "much, much worse" can have on an employee, the chapter "It's Not You, It's Me—No, Really" addresses some of these themes, including when harassment evolves into assault. Please be warned that anyone who has previously experienced harassment or assault themselves, or watched a loved one experience it, may be triggered by the contents of that chapter.

Keep an eye out for Office Creepers and even more for behavior that seems to be escalating. I wish you and your colleagues an abundance of safety and support in your career journey.

14.
MID AND END-OF-YEAR REVIEWS

The company you work for more than likely has some sort of performance review cycle in place. If I had to guess, it would occur twice annually. You will likely have mid-year and end-of-year (EOY) reviews with your manager.

I remember my first-ever review—how anxious I was for it, how much time and effort I poured into my self-evaluation portion of the review, how I lost sleep the days leading up to the 1:1 meeting I had with my manager to discuss their final review. I started working full time in January, so when mid-year evaluations came around in June I had been there the full six months. I was expecting an extremely thorough evaluation and was slightly disappointed when the meeting was not as grandiose as I had anticipated.

Not that my review wasn't thorough, but in my mind, the last six months had been extremely significant. I mean it was the first six months I had ever been employed full time! But just because it was extremely significant for me did not mean that my organization felt similarly. Time passes differently on the corporate clock; a year sounds and feels a long time in our personal life, yet might be a very standard frame of time in the corporate world. If folks are content waiting a full year to deliver a new product, imagine how these same people feel about your first six months of working. It's not that they don't care, but they may feel that not much time has passed at all.

By the six-month point your manager likely has a good inkling into the kind of performer you are, has been able to label you as "top talent" or "needs improvement," but given you are still so new to the working world in general, they might not approach your first-time review cycle with highly complimentary or highly critical feedback. This probably applies even more for new hires that enter a performance review cycle with less than six months tenure (for example, a recent graduate who starts their job in September and has an end-of-year review in December).

BIG DILL ENERGY

Don't call performance reviews a *pickle*, because they're not really *a big dill*. Get it? Bad puns aside, the truth remains: your first few performance reviews will probably be a huge deal to you but they might not be as significant to others, your manager included. Don't let that diminish your enthusiasm, but just be prepared that your review may not end up being the incredible awakening that you drum it up to be in your head.

I don't really know what I was expecting with my first performance review. I guess I was hoping my manager would sit me down in a conference room and confirm whether I was the next Mark Zuckerberg of business or if I was entirely incompetent and had made their past six months miserable. Even if they believed either extreme to be true, I highly doubt they would wait six months for my performance review 1:1 meeting to deliver that feedback. If you are graced with a good manager, they've probably echoed the sentiment of their review to you as time has passed instead of keeping feedback to themselves and waiting until mid/EOY reviews to share their opinion of you and your work. Which leads me to my next point.

SURPRISE ME NOT

You shouldn't be entirely shocked by the feedback your manager delivers in your mid/EOY reviews. If you are, that is a problem and you should work with your manager to understand how to better strengthen the existing feedback loop between the two of you. Whether it is a matter of your manager not clearly and consistently providing you with feedback, or you not understanding the extent of the feedback when it is delivered to you, performance reviews are a great time to figure out how these communication gaps have occurred and how to tighten them in the forthcoming months.

If you find yourself *positively* surprised by the accolades your manager has given you during this review cycle, congratulations. You might find yourself surprised because you are a bit too hard on yourself and naive to the quality of work that you deliver. Think about why that might be—and whether or not your ridiculously high level of self-criticism is harming you/your performance as an employee in any way. Having high standards for yourself is good, but if they are too high you risk not being able to unlock your full potential. It is hard to operate at your highest possible capacity if you are so self-critical to the point that you are unaware of what you are capable of. Finding the balance of having high standards for yourself yet high faith in your abilities is difficult; the sooner you begin exploring this balance with yourself, the better.

On the other hand, if you find yourself *negatively* surprised by the critiques your manager has disclosed during your performance review, be honest with them about your shock. You clearly haven't been able to read your manager's mind, which means they surely cannot read yours. They might not realize the criticism is a surprise to you, so it is important to find a way to tell them without appearing as if you are avoiding responsibility for your areas of improvement. I assume both you and your manager would much prefer for you to have a strong performance review. Therefore working together to figure out how you can set yourself up for that the next go around will be highly beneficial for both of you.

Managers are people too. Just like we as people might communicate and vibe very well with some of our friends and less so with others, the same goes for managers with their direct reports. Your manager might not tailor their communication strategies in a way that best supports your development and performance as an employee. Conversely, you might not have clearly articulated how you need your manager to package and deliver feedback so that you fully understand the extent of your performance in that moment (or lack thereof) and can action the feedback they've given.

As icky of a conversation it can be, it is necessary to do so right then and there. The sooner that you figure out what isn't clicking, the more likely you are to change the trajectory of future performance reviews. It can be a tricky conversation to navigate, so here are some phrases that you may be able to leverage when trying to get to the bottom of your surprise performance review:

"Thank you for the feedback. I was not aware that I was consistently [insert topic here]. How can we work together to identify this habit in real time so I can avoid making this mistake again?"

WRITE EVERYTHING DOWN

Documentation of events as time progresses is a repeated theme in these pages. It is an extremely important mantra to internalize and practice as early on as possible, because it applies to so many scenarios you may face while working. We've talked about never deleting emails in Part One, telling a friend or jotting down interactions with creepers in "Office Creepers," and now we're discussing the importance of documentation here in "Mid and End-of-Year Reviews."

It sounds counterintuitive for me to tell you how important it is to take the time to write everything down when you complete the self-evaluation portion of your mid or EOY reviews when I've simultaneously noted that reviews might not be a big deal to other members of your organization. Both messages serve different purposes and can coexist.

It is important to prepare your expectations going into your first several reviews. Just because they are special for you doesn't mean that it isn't business as usual for others. Regardless of how much people care about reviews in your organization, still taking the time to thoroughly document what you have accomplished during the past six months will help you build a paper trail of your contributions to the firm. These can come in handy should you find yourself in a situation a few review cycles in where you feel as if you were not promoted or awarded a progression in compensation as you rightfully deserved.

If you were to ever find yourself in a situation where you feel wrongfully recognized for your hard work, it would be much easier to pull your self-evaluations from previous cycles rather than trying to recall all of your important contributions from the past eighteen months in one sitting.

By taking your portion of the performance evaluation seriously and taking every tiny detail into account, you are possibly protecting your future self. Even if you don't have to pull up your paper trail to defend your right to recognition or awards, the documentation may come in handy for updating your resume, helping you prep for any panels you may be a part of and need to discuss your track record of excellence, etc.

PERFECT SCORES

I really hate being the bearer of bad news here. But let me forewarn you that the likelihood of you receiving a perfect score on your first *several* performance reviews is probably just as likely as you winning Gold in next year's Olympics. I get it—as a fellow perfectionist, this concept is extremely difficult for me to come to terms with. But if your manager were to award you with 5 out of 5 stars for every single competency you're evaluated on during your first few performance cycles, it would completely destroy your path for growth and scalability. It seems counterintuitive, but just because you aren't rated all 5's the first few times does not mean you aren't doing a kickass job. Promotion cases (and raises) are usually backed by a paper trail of continuous improvement and exceptional results. It would be hard to demonstrate this path and be rewarded with a promotion in a few years' time if you're starting from the very top after a single review. If you're ranked 5/5 to start, any exceptional contributions you make will look more like a plateau than a huge indication of growth (which is what you want as a fresh face in the corporate scene).

THE 1:1 THAT FOLLOWS

Writing your self-evaluation is only a portion of the overall review process. Typically your manager will arrange a follow-up meeting where you both discuss your portions of the review and their justification for whatever rankings they've assigned to you for each area you are evaluated. This is where you can ask your manager to clarify any discrepancies, ask for feedback on how to improve further scores, or voice any areas or skills you would like to explore the remainder of the year.

Because this time is completely focused on you and nothing else, you should take full advantage. It is easy for you and your manager to get absorbed in the day-to-day of business and defer topics like your personal development during your regularly scheduled 1:1 meetings. But the review 1:1 should be different: it should focus on you and only you. So be sure to walk into this conversation with a list of questions you have or topics you'd like to raise. The possible points of discussion you can raise are endless. They may or may not include some of the following:

- Share your interest in learning a new area of your team and ask how you can get further involved in these types of projects.

- Share your desire to be promoted; ask for insight into the timeline and for advice on what you need to accomplish in order to earn it.

- Ask for advice on how to identify and build strong relationships with mentors across the organization.

- Ask for their opinion on what skills you should continue to hone to have an even better review next cycle.

- Disclose concerns you have about the behavior of other employees (Creepers or otherwise).

NEGOTIATING

Negotiating is among the more awkward list of things that every entry-level employee will have to do at some point in time, especially for those who are not in jobs that frequently require this skill to be exercised (e.g., recruiting, sales, supply chain operations, vendor management, etc.).

Negotiating (or self-advocacy in general) is similar to going to the dentist. I find that some sickos like myself love a good trip to the dentist: getting the plaque from your teeth scraped off, the tools that vacuum out all the moisture in your mouth, the weird whitening paste that tastes funny, the whole nine yards. Whereas others struggle to bring themselves to make an appointment once per year, much less the recommended three times per year because they hate going that much.

The crowd is split just as equally when it comes to negotiating salary with your boss. Some people love every bit of it: the adrenaline that comes with presenting your case, the endorphins you might experience if the conversation goes well, the opportunity to voice your wants in return for all the hard work you've done over the past year. Whereas others dread the very thought of bringing up salary in a 1:1 with their manager and sweat through every second of the conversation.

No matter which side of the fence you fall on, there will come a day when you have to drop the S-word (salary), so you should try coming to terms with the idea sooner than later. Hopefully some of the points below will help you do so.

NORMALIZE NEGOTIATING

Because I am a former recruiter, many of my friends ask me questions they have regarding HR topics, specifically recruitment and salary negotiation. The most frequent question they have is "When a recruiter asks what my salary expectations are, what should I tell them?" I give them the same response every time: "Be honest." I would extend the same advice to conversations around salary with your direct manager during performance review season.

Talking about your level of satisfaction with your current salary and your desired increase at the end of the year isn't a trick. It's not like your boss is waiting for the day you bring up the S-word to say, "*Gotcha! I knew you'd bring it up—you're fired, you ingrate.*" The goal for entry-level employees is that a year into their first full-time role, they've slowly begun to come into their own, evolved past being "the new kid," and are now flourishing as a powerful force within the team. If you follow that path or something similar, it is fully understandable that your compensation would shift to reflect how your skills and contributions have shifted too.

Somewhere in the history of corporate life, bringing up salary was given a bad rep. The way that people still to this day tiptoe around even using the word "salary," one would think that it was downright profane, up there with every other swear word in the book. This has proven to be incredibly damaging, not just on an individual's psyche but on our society as a whole. Hesitancy that has been bred for decades around salary-related dialogue has had a severely negative impact on the wage gap that our society is desperately trying to rectify. Some companies have gone as far as publishing salary data on a quarterly/annual basis to increase transparency. It is becoming increasingly common to see compensation bands posted within a job description on LinkedIn. If companies are openly encouraging transparency around numbers, you should feel calm and empowered to do the same.

I say all this in hopes to silence that little voice that might be gnawing at the back of your head, telling you to be scared to bring up compensation during your performance review season. It's not only acceptable to bring up compensation, it's healthy. It contributes to the normalization of numbers, which has a positive downstream impact on issues like the gender wage gap.

REFRAME THE CONVERSATION

It's all about how you frame the conversation. If you approach the conversation in a manner that is ungrateful, intolerant, and demanding when you bring up your current salary and the raise you'd like to receive at the end of the year, that's exactly how your manager will perceive you. On the contrary, if you approach the conversation in a direct, relaxed, understanding, and inquisitive manner, that's exactly how your manager will perceive you.

Like most difficult conversations, it's all about how you choose to tee up the conversation and the manner in which your words are delivered. I've always found success in framing salary-related conversations as a question. Asking, "If I hope to *earn* a salary increase at the end of this year, what do I need to deliver and/or improve upon in order to achieve my goal?" or a similar variation. Using the word "earn" rather than "get" or "receive" or, worst of all, "deserve," is always a strong way to frame up comp conversations because it brings the ownership into your court; you are signing yourself up for a remaining year of hard work rather than asking when you're going to "get" a bigger chunk of change.

RIP OFF THE BAND-AID

The sooner you have the conversation, the sooner it will be over. As awkward as it can feel asking your manager about money, keep in mind they're not always the primary decision makers. All organizations have members of the HR function whose role revolves around compensation. They ensure increases are allocated fairly and resources for bonuses, for instance, are distributed equitably across the organization. This might work for or against you.

When it works for you, the compensation team might flag you as someone who deserves a bump in pay during the next cycle (reasons for this vary but could be along the lines of awarding their "high potential junior employees" as incentive to stay, ensuring your pay remains in line with people performing the same role, etc.). When it works against you, it might be a matter of your manager advocating for a significant increase in base salary but the compensation team denying the request due to a shortage in funds for annual performance awards. While it sucks when a salary increase is out of your manager's hands in such situations, hopefully knowing that they are not the only decision makers may reduce any nerves you have around using the S-word in your next 1:1 meeting!

15.
SHITTING WHERE YOU EAT

Shitting Where You Eat (SWYE)—what a brilliant analogy for such a beautifully complicated subject matter. This is one of those very controversial topics that most people determine a very cut-and-dried position on based off of whatever high-level threshold of moral standing they believe themselves to have. People likely hold a general mindset of "this is bad" or "I don't much mind" when it comes to coworker canoodling. You probably have made your mind up here yourself. But like anything in life, it's easy to think through which side of the controversy you stand on as an outsider, but your rationale may change the minute you experience it firsthand.

Some may still hold to their stance with conviction regardless of whatever individual nuances an inter-company relationship may have. Whereas others might be more open to being convinced that an inter-company relationship is OK as long as it does not involve a reporting line, direct peers, power dynamic, etc. For those who are a little more liberal when it comes to colleague relations, different tolerance thresholds of acceptability may still exist depending on the details of the case. For instance, slight flirting may be acceptable and unavoidable in some folk's eyes, but should two colleagues cross over into the realm of physical touch or, god forbid, infidelity . . . it's game over. They're both tacky (or probably referred to as much, much worse).

The irony is that whether you love or hate Shitting Where You Eat, if folks are presented with a SWYE scenario within the appropriate context, they may justify or even support it. This is perfectly illustrated by some of pop culture's most beloved TV characters and relationships. Sure, it makes sense that people are infinitely quicker to cheer on even the steamiest of relationships that develop between colleagues on-screen than they are in real life. One is fiction and one they might have to sit across from and witness day in and out, without the luxury of being able to turn it off by signing out of their Netflix account. But still, these fictional relationships are not far off from what goes on behind closed doors in real corporate settings. Therefore I find it odd that we can binge-watch one version while strictly condemning the other.

Whether or not an individual is comfortable with the high-level concept of coworkers gettin' it on in real life is one thing. Peel that macro judgment back a layer, and regardless of whether an individual gives SWYE a thumbs up or thumbs down, you can guarantee that many micro judgments are likely to follow. In short, Shitting Where you Eat is very judgy territory.

There is fat chance to no chance of someone being supportive of anything we witnessed Don Draper do throughout *Mad Men*. Alas, when we are at home watching *The Office* for the twelfth time over, we completely justify Pam and Jim's relationship because they're precious and perfect. They're "meant to be" and we cheer them on the entire time they "shit where they eat." Yet when it comes to Dwight and Angela, we may be more likely to condemn them for dating (and/or sleeping) with one another because the thought of them doing so is somewhat repulsive. They are not perceived in the same sparkling light as Pam and Jim; they are not the crowd favorites. Similar judgments, no matter how wrong, can be drawn when this unfolds in the workforce. These judgments can be made about couples as an item or, even more unfortunately, about the individuals by themselves.

I will never tell you how to live your life or what choice to make. It's not my place to tell you what to do and it surely is not my place to judge whatever it is you choose. This chapter is not about whether you do or do not SWYE. It is about knowing how to protect yourself should you encounter a SWYE scenario. Preparation and protection are major themes of this book. It felt important to uphold my commitment to them in this chapter especially, having lived, breathed, and experienced the cesspool of corporate gossip for myself. Because regardless of what you've seen on TV, what worked (or didn't) for your best friend and their hot date of a colleague, or what whispers you've heard about the things others in your firm have done, the *only thing* that matters when making the decision whether or not to engage in any canoodling should be: *Is this a safe choice for me?*

You are a bright, beautiful, budding new force in the professional world. It doesn't take a rocket scientist to realize that our generation holds aggressively different opinions when it comes to sex, love, and rock and roll. Some of the older generations, many of which will be your bosses and/or team members, will not be as liberal as Gen Z may be when it comes to falling in love and lust in a corporate setting. They may hold the popular opinion of "there are thousands of fish in the sea—find a fish that isn't employed here."

And I get it—it might be really, *really* difficult to do that, when you so badly want the "fish" that is the tall glass of water in a blue tailored suit on the seventeenth floor, who never fails to flash you a cheeky smile when you pass him as you walk toward the snacks every day. As evolved as we are in some ways, at the end of the day we are still animals with primal instincts. Some are better at controlling their urges than others, sure, but we'd be fools to not acknowledge that we all get them, even in a work setting. It makes total and complete sense to fancy your colleagues because we spend so many hours stuck on a floor (or in Zoom videos) with these people week in and week out.

CANOODLING CONSIDERATIONS

Because we like to be prepared for as many things as possible here, I've thought a step ahead and provided you with some crucial considerations to undertake if you find yourself slipping into a canoodling circumstance.

ASSESS YOUR RISK

The canoodling matrix provided is a great place to start when assessing your risk. Your risk assessment should be as comprehensive as possible; not just considering the risk of the acts of canoodling themselves, but the level of risk of canoodling in your organization in general. Is it easy to keep things quiet? Even if it's not, do people gossip/ judge harshly when other people are caught in a SWYE scenario? Or is your organization a bit more lax when it comes to these sorts of things? This is a great context awareness exercise for you to do ahead of making your final decision.

ESTABLISH PERSONAL BOUNDARIES AND COMMIT

What lines are you comfortable with crossing? What degree of inter-colleague relationships is totally off-limits? Think about this objectively before you find yourself caught in the midst of flirtatious temptation, because that can bias even the most logically sound individuals. Think about where your high-level opinion falls on the canoodling acceptability spectrum as we discussed at the very beginning of this chapter. Write this down and hold yourself accountable no matter how difficult it may be. I think it's complete and utter bullshit, but reality is things like hooking up with colleagues may "tarnish" one's brand as a professional.

If you're confident that you want to succeed in a specific industry—take financial services, for instance—you'll quickly realize it's a relationships business. As big as a city like New York is, you'd be surprised how small the financial services circle is, and how many times I've interviewed candidates who know members of our sales team very well and vice versa. As unfair as it may be, simple actions like kissing your hot cubicle neighbor at the holiday party may come back to haunt you later. I'm not saying that should you end up getting drunk and doing that, it's going to be the end of your professional reputation. I just think the corporate world is more brutal than we initially realize, and people are quick to attribute one's hard-earned success to anything but the fact that they worked their ass off for it. People are quick to draw the conclusion that you got the promotion because you wear V-neck blouses or flirted with the people who comprise the promo committee, not because you're smart, capable, and put in more hours than anyone else in your organization.

People often assume this without any sort of proof or logical theory. God forbid these same Karens of the corporate world catch wind of your personal business that may/may not involve intimacy with a coworker. They'll love nothing more than to use that to pad their case. It's not right, but it happens all the time, and the potential downstream effects of a decision made in your early to mid-twenties are something to strongly consider.

CHOOSE YOUR PARTNER-IN-CANOODLING WISELY

All the above aside, should you still find yourself having a bit of fun with your work crush, be sure you pick a good person to canoodle with. Make sure it's someone who is equally aware of how corporate gossip spreads like wildfire and is equally as adamant about not becoming a topic of conversation. Ensure it is someone you know well enough to trust.

TAKE IT TO THE GRAVE

As tempting as it might be, don't tell your work bestie. Don't tell anyone you work with at all. Take your canoodling to the grave, because if nobody knows about it, did it even happen?

WAIT IT OUT

Nowadays it's not very common for people to spend the entirety of their career working for a single firm. That said, you may very well find yourself (or the individual at the center of your SWYE fantasy) moving on to a new company at some point in time. I am not necessarily saying you want to hold your breath for the day one of you chooses to resign, but I am saying that if you can defer letting your attraction flourish until after one or both of you no longer work for the same company, this is probably the ideal scenario.

Thinking back to the earlier examples of TV relationships, we see this storyline so often on screen because it frequently occurs in real life. Feelings, attraction, urges, are all inevitable, especially when locked indoors with the same intelligent and well-dressed professionals for forty hours each week. Some people engage in colleague relations and never find issue. In fact, I've worked with people who found their now wife or husband through work. I think that's a beautiful thing and will make for a great story to share with your future grandkids. If you seriously think you've stumbled upon the love of your life in your entry-level analyst program, do not let this book or any shit opinion anyone else may have stop you from embracing that source of joy.

However, do consider the consequences if the "Hot Toddy" with the hazel eyes and chiseled chin on your team *does not* turn out to be the love of your life and you break up, leaving you to now collaborate with your ex-whatever on high stakes projects. Are you going to be equipped to handle that scenario, should it unfold?

Additionally, it is key to understand that like everything else in life, some people may be under a microscope more closely than others. This type of unfairness is seen throughout many aspects of working in a corporate setting, but especially so in instances of people fooling around with their colleagues. These individuals that for whatever reason are unfairly placed on the chopping block more aggressively than other employees (who have also had their fair share of canoodling) might be subject to more judgment and unintentional consequences. Ask yourself if you are unfairly placed in this group. If so, that might make the act of Shitting Where You Eat all the riskier for you than the average person.

16.
IT'S NOT YOU, IT'S ME—NO, REALLY

All right, you've made it this far without too much vulnerability. Heads up, that all changes now. In this chapter we're talking about mental health.

I have anxiety and depression. I am on antidepressants as well as a sleeping aid (because when the doctor asks, "Do you have trouble falling asleep or staying asleep?" I reply, "All of the above!"). From conversations with my dearly beloved therapist, I believe my mental illnesses stem from a life event that unfortunately holds a powerful influence on how I process life—how I feel I fit into it and how I feel about what I am worthy (and unworthy) of.

I have received EMDR treatment (used largely in the military to treat PTSD/trauma victims) for sexual assault that occurred when I was a teenager. It took me nearly six years of first denial, then paralysis and crippling fear, until I was finally able to find the courage to confront my trauma head-on. I sure as shit didn't find that courage on my own either. I was forced into confronting my past in the worst way possible: via a phone call while I was at work.

Around 10:30 a.m. on a weekday I got a phone call from someone I hadn't spoken to in nearly four years. When I glanced down at my desk and saw the name pop up on my phone screen I knew it could be for nothing good. I grew up in a small town, so I know that in small towns people talk. I suspected the only thing this individual could possibly be calling to talk to me about was my prior assault. Naturally, I had a bit of a meltdown. And by "a bit," I mean I had to be escorted into a frosted-glass conference room by my manager because I was so shaken up by the call I couldn't even make it to the bathroom before the waterworks began. I was such a distraught mess that my manager was seriously concerned for my well-being and sent me home "sick" for the day.

Without going into too much detail, it turns out I was right. The individual who called was reaching out because two young women in my hometown had recently come forward, claiming the same person who assaulted me many years ago had been sexually harassing them. My name came up as someone who may have information or a story of my own to contribute. At this time, barely anyone knew about my assault—not the individual calling, not the majority of my friends, not even my parents. Very few were aware of what occurred to me six years prior. I had *wanted* to tell them for so long, but struggled with when and how. I was paralyzed with shame and fear for so many years; I desperately wanted to heal but was unable to take a step in that direction. To be honest, I had always hoped for a sign or an event to give me a nudge toward recovery. I asked for a nudge and was granted this phone call as a tremendous kick in the ass instead.

To this day, getting that call was one of the worst moments I have ever experienced. I felt completely out of control. All these suppressed memories and emotions erupted out of me, without any time to prepare myself. I felt extremely violated. Work was a safe place that I poured my heart and soul into in order to distract myself from realities like this one, and the past's pain presented itself in my place of work without my permission. I also felt back up against a wall and the clock. The way our hometown gossip ran, I was sure my parents would eventually hear about it. I wanted to be sure they heard my story *from me* before they caught wind through the grapevine.

I began what felt like the Tour de Shame, calling my mom, dad, and siblings to let them know what was going on. I then told my roommates because we lived in a literal shoebox together at the time, so they'd no doubt hear my uncontrollable sobbing and know *something* was up.

I then had a big decision to make: whether or not I was going to join these young women by sharing my testimony. I needed time to think clearly, and frankly, needed time to recuperate my energy because I had none left to give this earth after the phone call parade.

On top of all of this, I had a workweek to finish. How the *hell* was I going to manage that amid a crisis? The thought of going to work, conversing with my colleagues, and interviewing candidates in this grave condition was mortifying. I was so desperate and distraught that I had no other choice but to call my boss and be honest. I straight up gave her the whole truth, in all of its pain and ugly. I told her I needed some time and was happy to take it from my vacation days. I just couldn't bear to finish out the week given what was going on.

And you want to know what her response was?

She was understanding. She recognized that this was a real and very serious situation, and was happy to grant me the time I needed to get my head in a better place before returning to work. She asked if it was okay to inform the head of our team of what was going on since my short leave of absence was so abrupt, and I was okay with providing the necessary level of detail in order to be excused for a few days. Much to my surprise, the head of our team went as far as to organize medical leave to cover the few days I was out so I didn't have to dig into my PTO allotment. She even gave me a personal call while I was out to check in and see how I was doing and if I needed anything.

These gestures meant the world to me.

I am *way* oversharing with you right now for two primary reasons:

1. To provide personal testimony as a reference point for when you interact with others in your workplace.

2. To provide personal testimony as a reference point if *you* ever experience, or are currently experiencing, something similar (and god, I hope you do not ever have to).

HOW MENTAL HEALTH MANIFESTS AT WORK

I am one year into consistent therapy and treatment for my assault trauma and still have barely scratched the surface on unpacking what occurred and the follow-on effect from it. Extensive therapy. Medication. Coming to terms with the label "trauma victim" and "trauma survivor." This is my reality. It is what it is. Whether there's trauma stemming from sexual assault or something entirely different, you likely have your own reality stemming from your past. And all our colleagues have their versions. What I'm getting at here is that pain and tragedy, no matter how big or small, doesn't just evaporate when arriving to work every day. Even if one is perfectly professional and polished, these realities are always operating in the background, demanding attention and energy. We all juggle doctor appointments with deadlines. We try new antibiotics while nervous about waking up for the big meeting the next morning. We anxiously await a medical diagnosis while giving the next big pitch to important stakeholders. Life does not stop for your work calendar and vice versa. If anything, the sick joke of it all is that when life ramps up and demands your focus, your Outlook calendar seems to join in on the fun, kicking you while you're down.

So, what's my point?

It may seem obvious, but it's worth calling out explicitly: personal events, traumas, and burdens all trickle into work. The real-life-heavy-shit is largely responsible for who we are and how we show up in all facets of life, professional settings included. Our traumas and hardships shape the type of employee we are, how we present in the workplace, how we think about problems and solutions, and how we engage in not only conflict but also conflict resolution. It is not limited to influencing our mood for a single day or affecting our attention span in a single meeting. Unfortunately, just as these events shape us at our core and have a long-lasting effect on our personal lives, they also impact us as professionals.

My lack of self-worth, stemming from a traumatic event that I am still struggling to come to terms with, makes me the employee I am today. My anxiety and irrational thoughts drive my productivity and attention to detail, as I am constantly operating out of fear of making a mistake. I present as "on top of my shit" to my colleagues because I am constantly trying to outrun my fear of proving myself right (that I am not worthy, I will always be and feel like nothing, I am stupid, I have tricked everyone around me that I am "good" when in all actuality I am "bad"). I consistently go above and beyond on my efficient delivery and quality of work in an effort to prove myself wrong (showing myself I *can* be good at something, that I am smart, I am capable).

Simple mistakes like flubbing in a meeting or forgetting to follow up on a task send me off my rocker because I unintentionally tie so much of my self-worth to my performance as an employee. I often find myself getting defensive over simple questions via email, as my security in who I am as an individual is mixed up in my output as an employee. Questions (even when innocent in nature) threaten my very existence, as not only an individual contributor, but as a human being.

On the contrary, accolades and positive remarks cannot help bring me back to earth. Positive performance reviews or compliments from stakeholders I work closely with have no lasting impact. Always genuinely appreciative of the compliments, I say "thank you" and accept the feedback, but it never really lands. No lasting impact is made internally, and my same toxic self-thoughts remain unmoved. I continue to build a case of reasons to hate myself from both sides of the fence—which, in turn, puts me in the position of *"It's not you, it's me; no, really"* for any and every "off day" I have at work.

No matter what experiences may be behind *why* what I've just said resonates with you, know that you are not alone. You may be surprised at how many people struggle to manage similar anxieties that impact their professional behavior.

MANAGING MENTAL HEALTH

If I could go back in time, I would have done the really hard "self-work" much earlier than I did. I certainly would have benefited from hearing someone speak freely about such topics as seeing a therapist, understanding more about myself, better anticipating how my mental health would manifest in a professional setting, identifying workplace triggers, and establishing boundaries. In that spirit, let's explore how to manage mental health struggles while working. Note: these are things that have helped me – they may not suit you, and that's perfectly okay. If that's the case, leave 'em!

FIND A THERAPIST

I've heard before that seeing a therapist is similar to going to a workout class. It's best for our health when we treat it as a preventative measure, rather than a reactive measure. It's easier to consistently work out and eat well in order to *not* gain five pounds than it is to lose five pounds *after* you gain it. Similarly, it's easier to consistently see a therapist so we have the tools and self-knowledge to prevent a mental health crisis than it is to pick up the pieces following a mental health crisis (trust me on this one). Let's normalize having a therapist and seeing a therapist even when "nothing is going on." It's healthy!

CONSIDER MEDICATION

I went back and forth for *months* on whether or not I wanted to start antidepressants. No amount of personal testimony I solicited from friends or reassurance from medical professionals could make me feel more comfortable about turning to medication for a solution to the symptoms of depression and anxiety I was experiencing. Slowly these symptoms began to aggressively impact me at work, to the extent that my anxious thoughts would elicit physical reactions during meetings. My stomach would throb and I'd nearly vomit after presenting just a single slide during a quarterly reporting call. I'd turn hot and red, and start to spiral down a rabbit hole of how awful I just did and how much of an idiot the audience probably thought I was. Five seconds later, no shit, I'd get an IM from my manager telling me how great my portion of the presentation was. My anxiety was making me borderline delusional. It was time to try medication. And I am very grateful that I gave it a chance.

PRIORITIZE YOU

Just like you can catch strep throat and be unable to work, you can wake up with increased symptoms of depression (or other mental health issue) and be unable to work. Prioritize your mental health as often and to the same extent you would your physical health, and don't feel bad for doing so. You aren't going to be firing at all cylinders if you are unwell emotionally, mentally, *or* physically. Leverage sick leave if you have to. Take care of you and don't let deadlines and projects deter you from doing otherwise. I am sure they can wait; you are worth it.

MITIGATE TRIGGERS AND BURNOUT

You may already be very in-tune with your emotions and can rattle off a list of actions or scenarios that may be triggering and/or emotionally exhausting for you. Others may not be there yet, and that's perfectly OK. If you are one of the former group, keep a list of possible triggers, along with steps you can take to set boundaries that will mitigate the possibility of you crossing paths with these triggers in your workplace. If you are more of the latter group, this is when finding a therapist to help you work through your past "stuff" might come in handy. You don't have to start at the very beginning of time (I know that seems daunting). You can always bring your therapist a list of things or situations you find yourself exceptionally sensitive to in the workplace and work backward from there. Therapists are great at being given symptoms and tracing them back to the root cause. Once you're there, you can begin developing your trigger contingency plan.

FIND SOMEONE TO CONFIDE IN

Find someone in your organization that you can lean on. Even if you do not feel comfortable disclosing a high level of detail, identify a person you feel safe informing that "something is going on at home" and leave it at that. Knowing ahead of time who within your firm you could go to in a time of need will be helpful should something (and I hope it does not ever come to this) end up erupting. This could be someone in HR, your manager, a peer, someone in another team who mentors you – anyone you trust. For me, this person was my manager.

Being able to confide in at least one person when life unfolds beyond what you can control will give you some breathing room at work. Someone will then know a bit about what is going on and can speak on your behalf if others ask if/why you are "off"—not to mention, it's a relief knowing someone is aware that life is just really fucking difficult at the moment. So no, you don't want to be the bubbly Brooke you normally are that day. And that's OK. Which brings me to the final point below.

KNOW YOU'RE NOT ALONE

You work alongside other human beings, who all have their own families, their own friends, their own marriages, their own children, their own stories and all of the ick and pain and hurt that may come with that. The moment we understand that the inevitable caveat of being professionals in a corporate organization is that we are *all human beings*, we can all breathe a little bit easier. We can take that mental health day when we need it without crippling guilt for doing so. We can avoid topics at the lunch table that might strike a chord with someone who has recently experienced a tragedy. We can be more understanding when someone reacts sharply or seemingly out of turn during a meeting. You are not alone. And by being vulnerable and honest about what is going on, you might just let someone else know that they're not alone either.

* * *

Now that I'm in a different place in life, I realize I wasted so much energy suppressing bad moments and fighting against negative self-thoughts. Had I learned proper strategies for managing my mental health sooner, I could have repurposed so much energy into being a healthier, productive employee who could properly disconnect and be a healthy, productive friend/family member. There is a reason that "acceptance" is considered the first step and often is considered the most difficult. Believe me when I say it was a long, exhausting, and painful process to:

- Confront my reality and circumstance, generally.
- Confront the reality of my behavior as an employee, specifically.
- Observe and evaluate how the two realities interacted with one another.
- Put boundaries in place and practices into action that have helped me mitigate my harmful behaviors and lean into my positive behaviors.
- Come to a better place of understanding and forgiveness with myself, and not kill myself (literally) with work.

The sooner that I could have accepted these truths about myself, my circumstance, and how it bled into the haven I created for myself at work, the better off I would have been for myself and others. I encourage you to dig deep, rip off the psychological bandage, and launch into the really, *really* hard—yet important—task of "self-work" required to address any big scary personal events. And do it on the front end of your career, rather than wait until you reach a breaking point and are forced into cleaning up the mess (like I did). I realize I could not have done my self-work to date without an amazing therapist, access to resources through my employer's health insurance, extremely understanding and supportive bosses, and perhaps most importantly, friends and family who listened to me and encouraged me throughout every step of the way. I do not take these privileges for granted.

* * *

If you need help, here are several different types of resources you can lean on for support:

Crisis Text Line
Text HOME to 741741

National Suicide Prevention Line
800.273.8255

The NAMI Helpline
800.944.NAMI

Safe Horizon: Rape & Sexual Assault Hotline
1.212.227.3000

TalkSpace

talkspace.com

Calm App

calm.com

BetterHelp

betterhelp.com

60 Digital Resources for Mental Health

by Social Work License Map

https://socialworklicensemap.com/social-work-resources/mental-health-resources-list/

Mental Health Resources

by the American Counseling Association

https://www.counseling.org/knowledge-center/mental-health-resources

17.
WITH ALL DUE RESPECT

It's okay—in fact strongly encouraged—for you to stick up for yourself when you're first starting out in an organization, although it might not feel that way. Trying to find your footing in a corporate environment can be difficult enough as a new employee without the added layer of complexity that toxic colleagues may bring to your cubicle. If someone is consistently causing issues for you, especially early on in your tenure, you may feel like the most appropriate course of action will be to shy away from confrontation, internalize the insults or belittling behavior, accept your fate, and keep quiet. You may think that if you follow these few steps, people will look at you in a positive light for being "mature enough to not entertain the drama" or "strong enough to move past" whatever is thrown your way.

This could very well be the case. But to play devil's advocate here, if you are consistently victim to a colleague's poor behavior and other members of your organization are caught in the crossfire, they may begin to feel uncomfortable and wait for the day you stick up for yourself. What might be intended as "being the bigger person and ignoring the commentary" may devolve into you not having the courage or self-respect to address the issue at hand. You can and will earn just as much (if not more) respect from your colleagues and superiors by appropriately addressing situations of disrespect in a productive manner. Calling out others' toxic behavior can seriously increase your clout. And it might just send the message to workplace bullies to back off from you and any other potential future victims.

However, I want to be clear that asking someone to stop a certain behavior, or pointing out to them that something they did was adversely harmful to you, should be done because you and *only you* want to do it. Perception is reality, especially in the working world, so being cognizant of possible perceptions your colleagues could draw in these situations is useful. But you should not only confront someone because you think it will impress your colleagues/superiors and vice versa. Nor should you remain quiet due to the same rationale.

So how do you determine when it's time to speak up? And what is the best way to speak up when having the "With all due respect, please cut it out" conversations? No one can answer that but you. You know your colleagues and workplace culture better than anyone else. You also know how much nonsense you can and are willing to tolerate. You'll realize some situations are just sheer pettiness (perhaps more worthwhile to ignore) versus when someone is saying something that is more damaging to your reputation, feelings of safety, and productivity (and therefore needs to be stopped).

You will know what to say and when to say it when the time comes to do so. Trust yourself. And if you aren't convinced, you can always review your plan to address any interpersonal conflict with your manager or a member of HR *before* you act. At the end of the day, if you do happen to miss the mark when gently pushing back on someone, own up to it and resolve your mistakes. But for the sake of not just leaving with an ambiguous *"follow your intuition"* or *"you'll know when you know"* as glamorous bits of advice, I have outlined a few common areas in which you may find yourself needing to stick up for *you*, as well as possible routes for resolution.

SHARING ISN'T ALWAYS CARING

The expression "sharing is caring" is great for someone trying to decide what to do with a box of cupcakes, but not so much for someone who just majorly fucked up at work and doesn't want to be the only person who goes down for it. It is not uncommon for an employee to pass off a portion, if not all, of the blame to their colleagues after they've made a mistake. It may or may not be done intentionally. Think back to "The First Fuck Up" chapter—admitting ownership of slipups, no matter how large or small, is difficult. It's possible that someone is struggling with the art of owning their mistakes and in their desperate attempt to stay afloat while admitting they messed up, they reach out for a life raft and end up bringing you down with them.

Lucky for you, however, you have read this book and understand the difficulty of admitting fault early on, as well as the possibility that you could be caught in the crossfire of someone who struggles with this. You understand someone might try to pass off some or all of their blame to you, and are prepared to act appropriately if this happens. The context and to what extreme someone tries sharing their responsibility with you will impact which course of action you might take to kindly push back on them.

ONE-TO-ONE

At least for me, this feels like the most appropriate way to address behavior eight out of ten times. The main reason I prefer 1:1

confrontation is the ability to avoid the opposing party feeling as if they've been "put on blast" in front of an audience. If an individual feels publicly attacked when you address their behavior, your message may be lost entirely. It could even exacerbate an already awkward situation. The risk of speaking to someone one-to-one is that there is no one else in the room to witness the exchange. It may be beneficial to err on the side of caution. For instance, if it's with a colleague you do not know as well or do not have a strong rapport with, or if the subject matter is particularly sensitive, a one-to-one chat may not be recommended.

If you do plan to address an issue with someone one-to-one, I always recommend telling someone (your manager and/or an HR team member) ahead of time and summarizing the conversation with that same person after the dialogue is had. This is a good countermeasure to put in place should, for whatever reason, the colleague you spoke with interpret the words said and resolution of the one-to-one differently than you did. Verbal summaries with your manager or HR team are great, but *written* summaries are even better. And doing it ASAP allows for greater accuracy.

JUST NIP IT IN THE BUD

Sometimes waiting to schedule a one-to-one conversation with the aggressor isn't as effective as addressing the poor behavior in real time. Or perhaps you already did have a one-to-one and the aggressor is resorting back to their old ways. If either is the case, it may be better to just *nip it in the bud*, regardless of whoever else is in the meeting room to witness. Common examples of where this conflict-resolution plan might be most effective are when a colleague is a repeat offender of:

- Making "harmless" jokes that degrade your intelligence

or competency (especially when said in front of other people).

- Saying passive-aggressive comments about past mistakes or decisions you've made.
- Outright microaggressions toward identities you hold.
- Taking their frustration out on you, rather than the issue you're discussing.
- Flat out ignoring your contributions during a meeting— either by not acknowledging what you say at all, or repeating your ideas as their own.

By calling out the aggressor in real time when the above situations (or anything similar) occur, you have plenty of witnesses. This immediately earmarks a point in time where you deemed the behavior unacceptable and voiced your concern. This is important should you have to build a case later on if the harassment continues. Another benefit is that it sends the message to others who bear witness that you refuse to be treated in this manner at the workplace. Informing a broader audience that you are not happy with that interaction allows for others to avoid making a similar comment toward you or any other employees in the future.

The major risk of calling an aggressor out in real time is the possibility of inciting a full-fledged argument; the individual may feel attacked and come back at you. If this person made the comment with an audience in the first place, they probably won't mind escalating the fight with everyone watching. If so, keep calm and shut down any further clapbacks with a "*I'm happy to discuss further offline; I don't think this is the appropriate place to continue this conversation*"—or something similar. This shows you are in control and not entertaining hostile antics.

KIDDING (NOT KIDDING)

Infusing humor into these sorts of tense conversations is never a bad approach. Not so much humor to where you can't effectively get your point across, but enough to take the edge off of things. Humor can be especially effective when calling someone out in real time with an audience present, as it brings lightness to the situation for all parties involved. I'll use a meeting I once held between a superior and my peer as an example. We'll refer to the superior in the conversation as Person A and my peer colleague as Person B.

I called a meeting to discuss the way forward about a particular initiative. Person A and Person B briefly derailed the conversation by discussing a project in deeper technical detail. I understand it's very easy and sometimes necessary to get off-track during a meeting, and what they were discussing was important, so I didn't mind the tangent. When the side conversation concluded and attention was brought back to the initial purpose of the meeting, Person B jokingly apologized to me for going off subject, as I "might not have kept up with what they were discussing because there were a lot of numbers flying around." For context, I was the youngest person on the call, the only woman on the call, and the *numbers flying around* were not anything extraordinary. Perhaps I was especially sensitive that day, but I didn't like the conclusion that I felt was being drawn: just because numbers were suddenly being brought to the table I could no longer understand the dialogue or provide value to the conversation. I absolutely adore Person B and fully believed he was well-intended with his comment, but still couldn't help but feel as if it was a bit degrading and in poor taste.

So what did I do? I *joked* right back with him, laughing and saying "Oh, I couldn't keep up because I'm incapable of processing numbers?

Yeah, *that* makes total sense." Person A laughed and made a joke about him making an enemy in me. Person B's face immediately flushed as he realized that, while unintentionally, he still managed to completely stick his foot in his mouth with that comment. Person B apologized immediately. By leveraging quick wit and humor, I was able to stick up for myself without causing any hard feelings.

PETTY IS AS PETTY DOES

Why grown adults feel the need to cause drama and "show their ass" (one of my favorite Southern sayings that basically means "act up") in the workplace is beyond me. There is a difference between teaching others to be self-sufficient and being petty. If you are trying to enforce self-service behavior by having someone dig for an answer like they are supposed to rather than feeding them the information, that is completely different than refusing to share an answer because you have some underlying bitter ulterior motive. I don't know *why* people are petty at work. All I know is that someone at some point in time *will be*, so you and all other entry-level employees should be prepared for it.

LET THEM KNOW THEY'RE WASTING TIME

One of my all-time favorite clap backs is some variation of "I don't think this dialogue is a good use of our time." If you remember back to Part One, I said, "Time is money and you sure as shit don't want to gain a reputation as someone who wastes either of them." This is exactly what being petty does—wastes time and money.

SMILE AND WAVE

As tempting as it may be to reciprocate, don't resort to their level of pettiness. Flat-out ignoring their small jabs and continuing to treat them with poise and professionalism will not only diminish the power of their petty remarks, but drive them nuts because what they're saying has no effect on you. It will also help you avoid getting sucked into a petty-fest and coming across as a hypocrite should you have already told them their pettiness is wasting the company's (and your) precious time.

SOMEONE SPEAKING DOWN TO YOU (OR ABOUT YOU)

This is a similar to someone being petty, but is ultimately a bit more hostile and direct. I think back to the time that a dear colleague of mine confided that a senior-level employee told them that the way I interact with people was "a sexual harassment case waiting to happen." Excuse my French, but I was fucking *livid* when this information was shared with me. I was pissed for a variety of reasons:

- The senior-level employee who stated this did so without me present to defend myself.
- The statement was beyond ignorant; my job was to make genuine connections with employees across the organization to effectively support their recruiting efforts. None of the relationships I made were inappropriate in nature.
- Ironically enough, the *statement in itself* was grounds for a harassment claim. How stupid can people be?

Regardless of how pissed I was, I decided not to do anything about it. I weighed the pros and cons of bringing the comment to HR and came to the conclusion that I didn't want to formally report it. Sure, it was a seriously stupid and toxic comment to make, but I did not want to deal with the possibility of it becoming a formal investigation. I mentally documented this as "Strike One" and should the same employee make a similar statement again, I would plan to address the situation then. I did not want to pursue action largely because I was not there to hear the comment firsthand.

A different example that comes to mind is when I had to be the messenger for a change in process that I assumed the colleague on the receiving end would not be happy about. Sure enough, the moment I shared the news of the process change, they snapped. The more I tried to listen and defuse the situation, the more frustrated the person became. When I realized things were beginning to escalate, I pulled out one of my favorite lines that a mentor taught me to use during situations like this: "*I understand you are frustrated, but you need to moderate your tone.*" I'm not saying it will always cause the person to pause, calm down, and apologize, but this time it did. Even if a one-liner like this will not rectify the situation, it is a strong way to let people know they are not allowed to speak to you in that way without you being disrespectful toward them and/or matching their hostile delivery.

Personally, I am more likely to act in situations where people are speaking to me directly because I am on the receiving end of their comments and able to shut it down in the moment. The first example would've been a game of he-said-she-said to understand *exactly* what was said and in what context before being able to address the problem effectively. Whether you choose to act on or ignore any situation similar to the ones shared above is totally your prerogative. There is no right or wrong when it comes to how you decide to react. By sharing these examples, it is not my intent to encourage you to address a situation that you don't want to. I offer them to give you support and affirmation should you decide that you do want to defend yourself. If a colleague of yours speaks down *directly to you* or *about you* in front of others, you have every right to defend your reputation. There are multiple ways to do so.

HANDLING IT YOURSELF

This is where the *"please moderate your tone"* applies. I know it can be scary, feeling as though you cannot stick up for yourself the same way you may see your colleagues do so just because you are "new" or "junior." This is imposter syndrome feeding us lies. While yes, we are new and learning, we are not any less of a contributing member to our company than our colleagues. As long as we continue to show respect to others, we deserve equal respect in return and should be empowered to ask for it when it is not given.

TELLING YOUR MANAGER OR HR

Even if you are empowered to speak up for yourself, you absolutely do not have to do it. I think having difficult conversations is an inevitable part of any career, and specifically corporate careers, so there is benefit to speaking to individuals yourself when their behavior warrants it. But at the end of the day you are new, learning, and may feel it's more appropriate to involve HR or your manager in helping with conflict resolution depending on the context. This is a great course of action and if it's how you feel most comfortable addressing colleagues where they're out of line, by all means, go for it.

NOT HANDLING IT AT ALL

This relates back to our first example. I grew up listening to my mom say, "You can't fix stupid," which I always found hilarious, but understood more and more with each year of age. Sometimes the best action is no action. If you feel that the party who has made the infraction is far beyond what anything you say to them will fix, you have the right to decide that it is not worth your trouble trying. It's not your responsibility to fix the way others act, so if you decide ignoring the situation is the best way to get peace of mind, then sit back and watch stupid be stupid.

WHEN SOMETHING PROMISED ISN'T DELIVERED

I often think new employees are so caught up in learning the new role, figuring out who they are and who they want to be, and being grateful for amazing opportunities, that they forget the street goes both ways. You are under contract—you do great work, you add value to the organization, you get paid for it. Employers are well aware that in order to keep great talent in this day and age, their end of the bargain far exceeds simply signing a check. Talented and hardworking employees need more than monetary incentives to stay in a certain position and/ or firm for a long time. These employees need to feel challenged, motivated; they need to feel they are being rewarded opportunities for further responsibility and growth. If you are graced with a good manager, they will speak to you about what growth looks like for you early on and often. They'll ask what direction you want your career to go in and/or listen when you bring it up with them.

Within reason, the firm should want to support your dreams and your desire to learn. If they don't want to, or are unable to support your desires in a reasonable amount of time (and that's not necessarily six months to a year), they should understand that it is likely you can and will find a new organization that does. Let's use a hypothetical situation to illustrate what I mean here.

Everett is eighteen months into his first job and itching for something new to add to his robust list of responsibilities. He has started to realize what aspects of his job he likes and wants to continue to grow in, as well as which areas he doesn't much care for. In hopes he can evolve from his current position to a different role on his team, he tries to *Become the Expert They Never Knew They Needed* by developing a business strategy for a huge area of need that has commonly been mentioned during weekly team meetings. This area of need does not currently have a formal owner, and no one has stepped up to the plate to assume the responsibility. It just so happens that this area of need is something Everett is passionate about and spent a significant amount of time studying during college. He feels that with the support and guidance of more experienced team members, he is the perfect man for the job!

Everett shares his business strategy with his manager and explains that he wants to throw his name in the hat to formally oversee the execution of the plan he's drafted. Because he has an awesome, supportive manager, they are pleased with his initiative and encourage him to present this plan to the head of the department. Prior to Everett's big meeting, his manager helps him refine his strategy and pitch deck.

Everett sits with the head of the department to discuss the plan he's put together and who he thinks he should partner with to execute the plan in the new year. He knocks the meeting out of the park! The department head is very impressed with Everett's initiative, makes a few tweaks to his plan and the other individuals he's listed that should be involved, and lets Everett know that he will play a key role in executing this strategy moving forward.

Everett is ecstatic. He feels that he has taken control of his career trajectory and the long, extra hours he put in to draft the business strategy has paid off. But as the new year arrives and weeks pass without any mention of the new initiative kicking off, he starts to get suspicious. Sure enough, at one of the weekly team meetings, the department head mentions that the new initiative is going to take flight soon and is being led by—wait for it—*not Everett*. It will be led by another member of the team who never before expressed interest in playing a role in this subject matter.

What the hell?! Everett is pissed, and rightfully so. Not only was he told he would be overseeing something and had the rug pulled out from under him, but the rug was pulled out completely to his surprise. He was not even given the courtesy of an "FYI" conversation before the changes were announced to the broader group.

What should someone in Everett's shoes do in a moment like this?

INQUIRING ABOUT THE CHANGE IN DIRECTION

It is okay to ask whoever in your organization (likely your manager or another mid- to senior-level manager) why there has been a significant change to what was initially discussed. I recommend approaching these discussions with a composed and professional mindset, focusing on the series of events, not your emotions. It's important to voice how misled you feel and how disappointed you are that you won't be overseeing the level of responsibility you were told that you would be. Having conversations about your disappointment in a certain outcome as it pertains to your individual development is important, because it flags throughout time where you've tried to grow as an employee and been unsupported or denied in doing so. Having specific points in times bookmarked can work to your advantage later on should you need to build a "case" for why you've made the decision to leave entirely (in the most extreme of outcomes).

DOING SOMETHING ABOUT IT

If situations like the hypothetical scenario we walked through occur frequently, maybe it's time to consider actions beyond just having conversations after the bait and switch. See the chapter "This Ain't It" for further detail on how to approach a career change should the failed promises push you there.

* * *

Setting achievable yet challenging goals plays an important part in obtaining successful results. If a goal is too easy, a team may not be utilized to its fullest potential and business opportunities may be left out on the table. On the contrary, if a goal is too challenging, the team may become burned out or discouraged before coming close to ever achieving it. This logic remains true at every level; it applies to individuals, teams, and organizations. This opinion is not exclusive to goals that are focused only on output or project deliverables; it is applicable to interpersonal goals as well.

Keeping this in mind, an entry-level employee should not aim to have *zero* interpersonal conflicts during their early career (or their career in its entirety). Not only is that "too challenging" of a goal, it's basically impossible. The inevitable part of human beings working with other human beings is that some degree of interpersonal conflict will arise. As we've just discussed, some conflict escalation can unfold unintentionally, whereas others arise due to deliberate action on the aggressor's part.

A more achievable goal for an entry-level employee would be *learning to appropriately manage interpersonal conflicts as they arise*, rather than aiming to not have any conflicts at all. This can be achieved by familiarizing themselves with potential situations that can arise and practicing how they would effectively resolve the particular conflict at hand. More importantly, this will only be achieved if the entry-level employee understands that their short tenure doesn't prohibit them from advocating for themselves.

It took me quite a bit of time and a manager that actively encouraged me to advocate for myself to reach this epiphany. Employees of *all* levels within an organization deserve the same amount of respect. Do not listen to the voice at the back of your mind that says you should brush off any snippy commentary or petty email exchanges. It does not matter if you're ten days into a job or ten years. If your colleagues' behavior begins to take away your power, diminish your credibility in any way, cause inefficiency and waste time, or frankly just get on your nerves, you are empowered to professionally tell them, "With all due respect, please cut it out."

18.
IT'S ALL FUN AND GAMES UNTIL YOU TEAR YOUR ACL

"*Expect the unexpected*" is such a good rule to live by, and is completely applicable to this chapter. As I write this, I am lying in bed wearing the same pair of sweatpants for the twelfth day in a row. My left leg is elevated in its knee brace, and I am binge eating cauliflower crackers because I have neither the energy nor motivation to prepare/eat real food. This is the last scenario I imagined I'd be in following my spontaneous ski trip to Park City, Utah. But the "unexpected" is often what the universe delivers, therefore *expecting it* is what we should all do in preparation for potential complete and utter chaos. In this case, the complete and utter chaos the universe so kindly delivered to me on a silver platter was what the medical community refers to as the "Unhappy Triad": a torn ACL, MCL, and meniscus.

What began as a crisp, bright January Friday in Utah turned totally fucked just after the third run of the day on the slopes with my close friend Alex. We had planned to ski for three days total, and naturally this occurred just two hours into Day One. I lost control on a rather steep part of the trail we were on and fell for what felt like ten solid minutes, hitting the side of the mountain at least four times before coming to a halt. My skis didn't pop off as they were supposed to, which is what I attribute my injury to. Yes, I am dramatic. And yes, I have an incredibly low tolerance for pain. However, this fall was really something special.

As soon as my body stopped I could feel that something was *very* wrong. I desperately flailed my ski rod in the air to flag down other ski pedestrians to call the snow patrol, who kindly strapped me into a toboggan and carried my pathetic ass down to the ski area's urgent care facility.

Two hours of pure hysterics, delirium, giggles, sobbing, X-rays, physical examinations, and only 600 mg of ibuprofen (not even the good stuff) later, I was out the door with a brace strapped to my knee, crutches in hand, and an assumed to be torn ACL (needing confirmation via MRI once I returned to New York). Not the sexy leopard snowsuit look I envisioned for my Park City weekend, but like anything in life, you focus only on what you can control, then adapt and find a way to still have a great time. Alex coined a great mantra that we abided by for the remainder of our time in Utah: *"We will only focus on what we can control. Our sobriety levels!"*

Thankfully, pounding mimosas and Mexican hot chocolate are activities that do not require full range of motion in both knees. Drinking is about all I could do in my injured state, so drinking is exactly what Alex and I did all weekend. We hit the town—crutches in hand, ibuprofen on deck—and managed to have a ridiculously good time meeting locals, scoring free drinks out of pity from others, shopping, inhaling delicious eats, and belly laughing 24-7.

Sure, I had a unique combination of severe knee pain and complete numbness throughout my leg. Fine, I was pretty concerned at the level of swelling in my knee, leg, and ankle. And okay, drinking probably wasn't the *greatest* idea at the time. But none of that mattered in Utah Utopia; those were problems to address when I arrived back in NYC.

The day following my return to NYC, I had an appointment scheduled with an orthopedic surgeon to confirm the suspicion of the ski clinic that my ACL was torn. I made it very clear when booking the appointment that I needed my left knee evaluated for an ACL tear, but the kind woman I spoke with on the phone for scheduling either misheard me or didn't give a flying fuck. Much to my surprise during my visit, the orthopedic surgeon informed me she only saw patients for hand injuries.

Thirty minutes of my life and fifty dollars for the visit copay wasted, I was annoyed, upset, and starting to feel desperate. My leg hurt, I was anxious for a formal diagnosis, and I put all my eggs in that provider's basket just to be incredibly disappointed. Fueled by frustration and in true, stubborn, Brooke fashion, I decided to take matters into my own hands and go to the ER. At the very least, I was determined to get painkillers because the over-the-counter ibuprofen just wasn't cutting it anymore.

It was all fun and games until I injured my knee. It was even more fun and games immediately following the injury while still in Utah. But back to reality in NYC, it was no longer fun, nor games. The non-fun and non-games skyrocketed the moment I checked into the emergency room.

Why? *Blood clots.*

I naively went to the ER assuming that it would be a quick trip, exclusive to my ACL. I would score some respectable painkillers to help manage my pain and swelling and if I was lucky, I'd finesse an MRI without needing a referral from an orthopedic provider. Needless to say, I got a hell of a lot more than I bargained for. Upon my arrival, the doctors were immediately concerned by my pain levels, swelling, and cold/numbness in my leg and foot. Little did I know that these symptoms of poor circulation far exceeded what was normal for a traditional ACL tear. After doing some imaging they found deep vein thrombosis (a blood clot) in one of the peroneal veins in my calf. Seven-plus hours on a hospital bed, an IV of morphine, and a series of tests later, I was discharged from the ER with a DVT diagnosis, a prescription for blood thinners, and instructions for where to go next to get an MRI for my ACL.

I now had a very long to-do list for the coming days: a series of "-ologists" I needed to contact and book appointments with, blood thinners I needed to take twice daily with food, things to do if I fell while on said blood thinners, bureaucratic hoops I needed to jump through in order to secure my MRI and obtain a formal diagnosis/surgery date for the ACL, etc. *What. The. Fuck.*

In other words, I was presented a full-time job of appointment booking and insurance navigation to do along with my current full-time job! How the heck was I going to make this work?

DEALING WITH DIAGNOSIS

If you didn't relate to the chapter regarding acceptance, diagnosis, and treatment of mental health–related illness, perhaps (again, I hope to god you don't) you will relate to *this* chapter regarding acceptance, diagnosis, and treatment of physical health–related incidents. While the two exist in completely different realms of health, the acceptance, diagnosis, and treatment processes are equally expensive, tiresome, and often frustrating. And they feel really freaking impossible to do when you work full time.

The universal truths I've come to realize for both mental and physical treatment/healing are similar. . . .

LISTEN TO YOURSELF AND GO EASY ON YOU

Regardless of the injury and/or diagnosis, there is an element of mental and emotional drain associated with physical ailments, and there is an element of wear and tear physically when you're dealing with mental or emotional ailments.

TIME IS NOW AN EVEN MORE PRECIOUS COMMODITY

A ridiculous amount of admin is required to book, keep, and follow up on appointments. Sometimes you just don't feel like fucking doing it. It's okay to feel this way (and vocalize it).

TAKING CARE OF YOURSELF AND YOUR ISSUES IS EXHAUSTING You'd

rather allocate your time to drinking with friends over attending doctor appointments, and allocate your money to Saint Laurent bags over surgery expenses. It's okay to be annoyed about this (and vocalize it).

THOUGHTS WILL CONSUME YOUR ENERGY

Whether it be about outstanding diagnoses, forthcoming surgeries, new medication, injury recovery, or upcoming appointments, thoughts about these events are always consuming energy by operating in the background, even during work, just like we discussed in the chapter regarding mental health. If this pertains to you, go easy on yourself. If it does not pertain to you, it likely pertains to a number of your colleagues. Go easy on others.

LIFE DOES NOT STOP FOR YOUR OUTLOOK CALENDAR

When shit really hits the fan and you get not only an ACL tear but deep vein thrombosis (blood clots), you have to find a way to take a pause. Be honest with your boss and your colleagues, and tell them what's going on sooner than later. I can't speak for every organization but vulnerability and transparency has never bitten me in the ass (yet). If you share the extent of what is going on, people will encourage you to prioritize your health—which is exactly what you should be doing.

Similar to when I hit rock bottom with my mental health, after leaving the ER I realized that if I didn't deal with this shit myself, it would never be dealt with. When I entered the terrifying chamber that is "*health rock bottom,*" I repeated the same level of emotional kicking, screaming, and temper-tantruming I did before I began seeing a therapist consistently a year earlier. After getting the woe-is-me out of my system, the "*fight*" in my fight or flight instinct kicked in. I rolled up my sleeves and hunkered down for what I did not know at the time would be a long, wild ride to ACL and DVT recovery.

WWBD? (WHAT WOULD BROOKE DO?)

As if ACL surgery and deep vein blood clots were not challenging enough to deal with individually, much less together, I had to sweeten the pot by adding a few environmental factors to the mix to further complicate things:

- I lived seventeen hours (drive) away from my closest family members. Therefore I was reliant on friends to handle all the good, the bad, and the ugly of the post-injury process. I eventually had to make the decision to move back in with my parents for the duration of my surgeries and recovery.

- In the words of Cher, *"I am a rich man"* in many ways, health insurance included. I shifted to my own health insurance plan immediately upon securing a full-time job. Don't get me wrong, I was/am grateful to have health insurance in the first place (great health insurance too!) but the immature twenty-three-year-old in me hated seeing money fly in every direction other than building out my Nike sneaker collection.

If you find yourself in a similar predicament navigating physical injury or illness while holding a full-time job, the following advice might help.

BE BRUTALLY HONEST

I talked about how liberating and sometimes beneficial it can be to share mental health struggles with HR or your manager in the chapter "It's Not You, It's Me—No, Really." I am going to repeat the same bit of advice here, and even go out on a limb to say it might be easier to share struggles regarding physical injury or illness since society stereotypically seems to extend empathy more quickly with physical health issues than they do for mental health.

Telling your manager what is going on can be especially helpful if you find yourself in a situation where you have been injured or diagnosed with an illness but are still navigating your timeline for treatment, surgery, etc. If your path to recovery remains ambiguous after your initial diagnosis, you might feel better being honest with your manager early on that you are not feeling well and will have a spotty availability moving forward as you go to the appointments required to solidify your treatment plan.

While I was waiting for the final verdict on my situation and how it may impact my work availability, I was transparent with my manager and team members and had their full support to prioritize my health/appointments first. My situation was fairly urgent at first. My teammates were patient with me as I scheduled last-minute appointments and were happy to jump in and help out with some of my usual duties as I had to miss more work than I would have liked. I found that being honest with them about my condition significantly reduced my anxiety.

Knowing my brain, I would have worried myself into a tizzy thinking about all the possible slacker-esque things my teammates might have been thinking about me should I randomly start taking chunks of time off throughout the work week for appointments. By being honest about my current circumstance, I got ahead of any faulty perceptions that could have taken place. No one thought I was "slacking," because they knew exactly what was really happening.

There is no convenient time to experience a physical injury or illness and most reasonable people will be understanding of that. You do not have to go into a great amount of detail with your condition(s) if you do not feel comfortable doing so, but providing a baseline of transparency with your manager or HR at the very least will help your team advocate for you and support you while you need to be absent.

DISABILITY LEAVE

Remember way back in Part One's "Benefits: WTF" where I recommended you pay attention during benefits orientation? Yep, this is why. You never know when you might need to make a lump sum of visits to the doctor, or even worse, take a portion of disability leave for your recovery. I was thoroughly confused on what to do when I needed to exercise medical leave, as I expect most people are. I recommend you lean heavily on your benefits expert and engage them early on when you realize you may need longer than one to two weeks to recover from a surgical procedure (to my knowledge, any recovery longer than two weeks requires long-term disability leave to be filed). I am not anywhere close to a benefits expert. I won't go into tactical advice here, but I will leave you with the encouragement that it's very hard to mess this up. I know it can be stressful needing to collate and file a bunch of paperwork from your medical professionals, but the third party that handles your leave will be there to help you along the way. I was surprised at how accommodating the third party org I worked with was with leave extensions—so don't stress if you're in a situation similar to mine where the path to healing is unclear for an extended amount of time. Leave extensions are manageable.

MAKE THE MOST OF IT

I absolutely hated when people said this to me after I first injured myself. I didn't want to make the most of anything, because I didn't want to be *in* this situation to begin with. As time passed, and I slowly came to terms with the fact that I had a lot going on and a long road to recovery ahead, I began to slowly entertain the idea of "making the most" of things. Are there new skills you want to learn but haven't had time to? Is there a book you've been wanting to write but haven't had the opportunity to do so? (*Wink wink.*)

Extended medical leave is a great time to critically think about who you are, who you want to be, what job you want to have, where you want to live, and everything in between because you really have no other choice but to think with all the time you'll have on your hands. During my medical leave I was able to reflect on my current employment status and what I wanted my short and long-term career trajectory to look like, as well as identifying what skills I needed to begin learning in order to achieve those goals (once I got to feeling better, of course).

* * *

Here I am six months following my tumble on the slopes of Utah and I am *still recovering*. As I write this, I am *still* undergoing rigorous physical therapy because I have not relearned how to properly walk without crutches. Insane, right? *It's been six months.* I have had a significantly more complicated series of medical events unfold than expected, and each event has continued to pose other issues or require follow-on surgical procedures. I am okay and in high spirits. I don't highlight this for pity; I highlight this to prove that timelines for recovery are extremely unpredictable and that serious medical issues can pop up for anyone at any age. As invincible as I used to believe I was, I have had a very humbling experience at twenty-four years young, knowing now that any of these medical issues are fair game regardless of an individual's age or physical fitness.

It's no secret by now that I am a workaholic. I've loved my teams and loved the roles and responsibilities I've held. The last position I expected to be in at this point in my career is exactly the position I've found myself in—three months strong on disability leave, still working through diagnosis and recovery. As a self-identified workaholic, I feel that I have more credibility than maybe some others would when I say to you: *Prioritize* yourself *first. Work can and will wait.*

During my Profreshional Year, I always operated under a "I'm Sick and I'll Prove It" mentality, doing things like showing up to work coming off of three days post–strep throat diagnosis, looking like the Crypt Keeper. Looking back now, I realize it was so stupid of me to not just use the sick day and stay home. Pushing yourself beyond your physical limits while you are sick and need healing is not noble or admirable; it is foolish. So take the sick day (or multiple) if you need to without the underlying fear that others may not believe you actually need to. Take the disability leave if it's available to you and you need it. And like we discussed in the "PTO" chapter, do not just take sick or disability leave but *really use it* whenever you do. Disconnect entirely to focus your energy on healing, not on what emails are coming through. Because as important as work might be to you, the reality is that nothing can be important to you when your physical health is not functioning as it's intended. If you are not in prime physical health, your output at work cannot be in its prime either. Take it from a fellow workaholic and Unhappy Triad/DVT survivor!

19.
THIS AIN'T IT

Studies show that entry-level employees will leave their first employer after 1–3 years on the job. The irony of this statistic is that while it seems most entry-level employees are on the same page about the longevity of their first employment opportunity, many of my peers have struggled to make a change when they were no longer satisfied with their current job and/or employer.

Of all the topics in this book, this one is especially important to me, because it seems to be a major point of stress for folks up to a few years into working full time. I have navigated several conversations myself during my own career change, as well as numerous conversations with close friends as they've navigated their career change journey. The dialogue seems to always be the same; regardless of how certain an individual is that they are not happy in their current role or organization, there is a high degree of angst and hesitation around seeking new alternatives. Which leads me to the burning question of: *Why do entry-level employees struggle so much with the internal dialogue that arises when they first begin to experience job dissatisfaction?*

Imposter syndrome is a bitch in every facet of life, but it is uniquely evil in the mind of a junior employee. Because we are so new to corporate life, we have no benchmark for what things actually are and what they could be. This adds stress when we are self-monitoring and trying to determine whether or not we are dissatisfied with our current job enough to make a change. It is impossible to know for sure whether or not we "have it bad" or if the things that annoy us about working are "just the way it is" in adulthood.

If you are anything like me, you are self-aware and overthink to a fault. You run yourself in circles trying to decide if you are actually unhappy in your current workplace or if you are just a stereotypical Gen Zer coming into the corporate world with grandiose, unrealistic expectations. Sound familiar at all?

Because everything is so new in your profreshional year, any of the above thoughts are completely valid when toying with the possibility of finding a new occupation. However, just because it is a *valid* headspace to be in does not mean it is the *correct* headspace. And it sure as hell is not a valid headspace to *stay in*.

I view the process of growing up and out of a job similarly to how we grow up and out of life. Hear me out. When we join our first company in an entry-level capacity, our clock is immediately rolled back to infancy. We might as well walk into our first day sporting a fresh pair of Huggies and sit at our desks with binkies hanging out of our mouths. Just like infants, entry-level employees possess a strong doe-eyed naivety and innocent interpretation of our corporate surroundings because it is all new. We may not even realize we possess these traits or perspectives until later.

This is why teams often love bringing college grads and new hires into their groups; they provide a freshness and positivity that the team may or may not be running out of, because unlike most employees within an organization, entry-level hires are not yet jaded and broken in. People new to the workforce leave their colleagues with the same refreshed feeling that a stranger's baby or golden retriever puppy may leave you with when you pass one in the park.

And because entry-level employees' clocks are set back to infancy upon joining an organization, they have a high tolerance for BS toward the beginning. The newness of it all hides what will eventually unveil itself to be a pattern of intentional behavior or organizational norms.

Just like kindergarteners may not always catch on that their classmate is being mean to them, the new hire may not realize that Suzy isn't really supporting their development as an individual—she just wants you to do her grunt work. The list of applicable examples is endless.

After the first 6–18 months of employment, entry-level employees begin to hit what I think of as F-TEP (Full-Time Employee Puberty). It's that same painfully awkward time most people experience in middle school when you start to realize what you like and what you don't like, and you may get an irresistible urge to explore things you haven't before. You begin to become more certain of yourself and reflect that in who you spend time with and what you produce. And it is the time you realize that, unfortunately, not all people are well-intended and they know full and well when they're being an asshole.

Keep in mind, F-TEP is just like normal puberty: *It looks different for everybody.*

For the cute sixth graders who started way ahead of the curve and already wore Abercrombie and Fitch their entire lives, F-TEP might be less life-altering. They may begin to establish their brand as a professional and make modest changes to their approach or outlook on work, but ultimately may still be content with the career path or organization they chose and decide to stick around for the long term.

However, if you were a quirky, obnoxious butterball of a sixth grader like me, who was saved by the changes puberty brought in seventh grade, your F-TEP experience may be a little more intensive and result in a complete 180. You might wake up one day a year into your first job and realize that what was once magic no longer aligns with your interests—which is completely normal and OK. It doesn't make the job requirements, your employer, your colleagues, or you wrong. It just means you've grown, which is incredible, and exactly what you should be doing.

Continuing with the baby/pre-pubescent teenager analogy, rapid change and growth isn't a surprise during your first 1–5 years of employment; it's an expectation. Every new word a baby says is an achievement. Every first date or first dance in middle school is equally mortifying as it is exciting because it's a series of firsts. Like babies and preteens, you enter the workforce extremely impressionable. Things like hearing the career path of a member of leadership in your organization or comparing 401(k) match benefits with close friends working elsewhere will cause you to continuously evaluate what options are out there and where you're at currently. It would be unusual if you looked, dressed, and acted the same now as you did in sixth grade. The same goes for if you acted and interpreted your work environment the exact same way three years into your first job.

All of that cringy analogy said, *why* in the world do entry-level employees still struggle so much when the new hire magic dims and they come to the conclusion that their current role, department, organization, etc. is no longer what they want? This chapter is for all those who find it difficult to act once you come to this conclusion about your current job: *This ain't it.*

WHEN I REALIZED MY FIRST ROLE WASN'T IT

As previously mentioned, I am a human resources professional by training. Sure, I have had exposure to general business management/operations responsibilities since the age of seventeen when I was promoted to supervisor (a year later, manager) and began running shifts at a local fast-food chain. But when it came to tasks or responsibilities I took on beyond the bare minimum of what was required to run shifts, I always aligned myself with HR-related duties. I oversaw the candidate application, selection, interview, and hiring processes. I helped plan and execute employee events and influenced reward and recognition–related policies within the franchise unit I worked in. I trained nearly all new hires, facilitating their new hire orientation as well as providing training on the job.

My draw to human resources–related work continued throughout my employment in college, followed me into my studies, influenced me to obtain a Bachelor's of Business Management with an emphasis in HR, and it provided direction for all corporate summer internships I applied for. I figured that I enjoyed business, and had a burning passion for people/human behavior, so why not marry the two interests with HR? My plan seemed foolproof; I was certain I was signing myself up for a lifelong career of enthusiasm and fulfillment.

Fast-forward to January 2019 when I began my first job as a recruiter at a medium-sized FinTech company. I loved my team as if they were my own family. And for a young adult who knew no one else in New York City at the time I relocated, they essentially *were* my family (and some still are to this day)—which made my decision to change roles within the company at the one-year mark of employment extremely difficult to make.

The honeymoon phase in my role as a recruiter lasted about four months. I loved my team, I loved my organization, and I especially loved the gorgeous four floors we held for office space in the New York Times Building. I loved planning and executing the same summer internship program that had groomed me for full-time employment the summer prior. I loved guiding the new class of precious interns through the magic that is a summer internship program in New York City.

But before I knew it, the two-month summer program quickly passed and I was thrown into a portion of my new role I had not yet been exposed to: university recruitment. Given the nature of my role and the recruitment cycle, sourcing and hiring talent was the majority of my job and it took me getting into the seat full time before that really clicked in my head. It also took me getting into the seat full time to actually recruit someone completely by myself, which was not something I was exposed to as an intern. And how could I have been? I was just an intern. It is understandable that not all facets of the job are going to be accessible until an individual joins a firm full time. This is very important to keep in mind during your own idealistic summer internship experiences.

I spent maybe eight months of the year sourcing and recruiting folks to join our program, and only about four months or so planning and managing the summer internship experience. Unfortunately for me, this did not align with how I enjoyed spending my time. I would have preferred to devote 75 percent of my time to program management and 25 percent to recruiting, but that just wasn't the way the cookie was going to crumble.

That fall I planned and attended five career fairs and barely kept my head above water trying to fill roughly two dozen internship roles within a four-month period. Needless to say, it was *a lot*. An amazing, fast-paced opportunity that I would not trade for the world, but all the same, it was pretty intense for twenty-one-year-old me.

On top of learning by fire during the grueling season that is fall university recruitment, the firm itself was shapeshifting faster than I could blink. The organization I joined as an intern in summer 2018 was no longer the same place just short sixteen months after I started working there. It wasn't all the firm's fault. Across the financial services industry, many firms were facing lower margins and seeing consolidation left and right. However, some incidents that need not to be named in this book, were the firm's fault. I was not happy with what events occurred and was even less thrilled with how my company handled them. I call out the two sides of this coin explicitly because regardless of whether the firm can or cannot take ownership of the events that have begun to rub you the wrong way, you are still fully empowered to come to the conclusion that *This ain't it.*

I've always loved the quote "we fell in love slowly, then all at once" because I think it hilariously applies to so many things in life. For instance, getting fed the fuck up with your job. You probably begin to get annoyed slowly, and then become irritated and completely fed up all at once.

So what did I do about it when I found myself in this predicament?

One of the beautiful things about recruitment, particularly in a small- to medium-sized firm, is that the job requires a high degree of cross-functional collaboration due to the need to partner with hiring managers all across the organization. This worked to my advantage when I realized recruiting *ain't it* for me, because I not only had strong rapports with hiring managers who had the ability to grant me an internal transfer if I proved myself valuable enough to add to their team, but I was also very close to the headcount process and knew when and how I would need to approach my scheme to transfer out of the HR department.

Around the same time that I was coming to the realization that recruiting was not the long-term gig for me, my company acquired a small fleet of data scientists based in St. Louis, MO. This small company we had just purchased brought a ton of extremely valuable data science expertise to the firm. Because I oversaw junior recruitment, I ended up working very closely with the founders of the new company as well as their lead data scientist to establish an on-campus presence at schools in the Midwest (which our company did not have to date) in order to support forthcoming hiring initiatives. I sort of fell into the unofficial role of the primary point of contact for the newly acquired team, becoming the main link this group had to the broader organization. I also developed very strong relationships with the new group of data scientists; they brought a new wave of start-up energy that our parent organization desperately needed. Working on filling their open data science roles gave me a sense of pride and purpose that had been slowly slipping away the further I found myself into the university recruitment season.

Beyond enjoying the people I was working alongside and the new aspects of my role, it seemed that I really had a knack for identifying data science candidates. Learning what made someone qualified versus not so much was interesting to me; I loved picking the team's brains on the tools, technologies, and projects they were looking for in prospects. I was excited when I identified a good resume, and even more excited when I seemed to explain the role/requirements with conviction to data science students. It was addictive. I felt "smart" for one of the very first times in my life. I myself did not have a technical background, yet I could somehow still help build and provide value to these extremely talented technical teams.

Then, seemingly both slowly and suddenly, opportunities for further collaboration with the data science team emerged. Part of it may have been my own creation, because I made sure to find a way to create opportunities for collaboration with this group since it was the favorite aspect of my job. But it was also largely due to me being the perfect person to jump in and assist when a more organic opportunity for collaboration arose. I had the strongest (and really *only*) rapport with this new data science team since their acquisition. What started as somewhat organic became a very intentional attempt on my part to become the Expert They Never Knew They Needed for the newest addition to my company's mergers and acquisitions (M&A) portfolio.

My responsibilities soon expanded from general recruitment–related tasks to higher-value merger and talent retention–related initiatives. I performed a gap analysis of what had been done and remained to be done from a merger point of view and crafted a detailed plan for resolution of the outstanding tasks.

For the remainder of the year I partnered with the data science teams and HR business partners to execute on this plan and saw positive results. After four months of close collaboration, nearly all outstanding tasks in my plan had been resolved, so it seemed my time working with the data science department was coming to a close. I was nearly devastated at the mere thought of it. My partnership with this group on paper was a supplement to my full-time role as a recruiter. It was an "extra," yet the part of my job I was most excited for and cared most about. I wasn't ready to let go.

So I expressed my interest in continuing to work with the data science teams to the department head during one of our regularly scheduled progress checkpoints. I said I thought now was the time to raise my hand, to ensure I voiced my interest before peak hiring season kicked off in the new year. I said I realized I had training specifically in HR and recruitment, but was confident many of the skills were transferrable to a role in project management, sales, business management, or any other opening the team may have that I may be a candidate for.

It sounds really simple, relaxed, and concise written in paragraph form in this book. That absolutely was not the case in real life. I am recalling the words I said as best as I can because the reality is that I nearly blacked out during this nerve-racking conversation. I planned exactly what I was going to say for weeks, and finally worked up the confidence to do it, mainly because I felt it was "now or never" in terms of timing. I fully talked myself through how I imagined the rest of the conversation with the department head would go—mainly some variation of

"How cute; I appreciate the sentiment, thanks, but no thanks."

Or *"Yeah right – no way you are qualified for any openings we have."*

Or simply *"Hahahaha. Hell no."*

But, entirely to my surprise, the department head was receptive. They said they were not yet certain what headcount would look like for the next year but we could continue to explore possibilities of roles the team may need.

From that moment on, it was game time. I patiently yet consistently propelled forward conversations around possible employment opportunities. I networked internally with other key stakeholders, expressing my interest in working for the data science department, asking for their insight and, ultimately, trying to obtain their blessing should I end up joining their team. I studied key data science concepts. I asked familiar faces within the data science department to walk me through their workflow and requested a list of tools and technologies I should begin to familiarize myself with. And most importantly, I continued to show up and kick ass in my role as a recruiter because I knew there was no chance at me trying something new if I wasn't excelling in what I was doing currently. I wanted this change with every fiber of my being. If it did not work out, it would have nothing to do with me dropping the ball.

I went as far as booking a "leisure trip" to London in January 2020 so that I could work from the UK office for a day and continue conversations around my internal transfer with key stakeholders in person. That might have been a bit insane on my part, but it was well worth the investment. If I have learned anything since graduating into adulthood, it's that no one is going to show up for you to a higher degree than you do for yourself. So if you think you need to book a flight to a different country to secure your dream role, why wouldn't you?

* * *

For the sake of wrapping up this story before this chapter becomes a novel of its own, I internally transferred from being a junior recruiter to a data science business manager just 18 months into my full time career. From initial inquiry to confirmation, it took three months of patience and dialogue before hearing that there was indeed an opening in data science and that I was being extended the position. It took three additional months of patience for me to find a replacement for my current role as a recruiter before making the official transition. Because I was eager to begin, I balanced both roles for those three months, averaging 12- to 16-hour workdays.

My story is just one example of the many different scenarios that can unfold as you not-so-suddenly are tired of your job and find yourself pouring into this chapter for validation. The ironic thing is no matter how many different ways someone can arrive at the conclusion that they want to GTFO, the imposing feelings of imposter syndrome that paralyze individuals from actually making the jump are often the same:

- "Maybe this is just the way things are everywhere, or maybe it's worse at other places."
- "I feel like I am ungrateful if I leave. I feel indebted to my current team/organization."
- "What if I don't have the skills to succeed in what I actually want to do?"
- "Looking for another job scares me. What if my current employer finds out and holds it against me?"

If the feeling of *"this aint it"* slowly starts to creep in and consume your every thought while you are working a job you once loved, listen to that voice and consider the remainder of this chapter a sanity check and empowerment to begin taking steps to make a change.

AFFIRMATIONS FOR WHEN IT AIN'T IT

I realize some of us may have stronger intuition than others. But at some point we are all capable of detecting when we are unhappy, anxious, fearful, cautious, being manipulated, or frustrated.

Some of us can analyze a situation and know exactly how we will react internally before events actually unfold, whereas others may need to take a few good smacks around until we are able to process, *Hey, I don't have a good feeling about this.* Whether it takes six months or six years to detect and appropriately diagnose what the root cause(s) of these emotions are, we will *all* get there eventually and are capable of addressing the issues at hand. Regardless of the length of time you're into a job, if you start to feel any of the above (or something different, but equally as negative), take it as a sign to explore other options. And try to avoid any feelings of self-doubt that may begin to cloud your thought process.

I think most of the awkwardness that comes with the decision to make a drastic change to your employment status is due to the fact that it's a totally new situation. Like navigating any big decision for the first time, it is difficult because you have no benchmark to refer back to when weighing your pros/cons. Each circumstance comes with its own set of stressors which makes it tricky to generalize advice for when you are faced with the decision to try something new. Whether it's the risk or the unknown of jumping to an entirely new industry, changing your reporting line internally, reputational risk associated with leaving, genuine regard and concern for the coworkers you are leaving, fear of failure in a new role, or a combination of the above, there are two key things to keep in mind:

- Everyone's decision to leave their current role is icky and stressful in the moment.
- Once you make the change and are on the other side, you're not going to give a shit anymore, I promise.

So as difficult as it is, take a deep breath and attempt to make your transition process as stress-free as possible, because if you died tomorrow the company you currently work for would keep chugging along and eventually have to find someone else to do your work. The same goes for when voluntary turnover occurs.

OTHER SCENARIOS THAT AIN'T IT

For me personally, the only thing that *wasn't it* was the role and responsibilities. I just simply realized I did not want a career in recruitment, and I wanted to make that change as soon as possible. In some ways, this made it painfully difficult for me to make a change, because I fervently loved my colleagues, my current manager, and the industry I worked in. But as painful as it was for me to say goodbye to my current team, I was willing to do it because the type of work I was doing mattered more.

Individuals are motivated by many different things. Something that "ain't it" to you may be a dream for someone else, and vice versa. We all come with internal tolerance thresholds (whether we set them intentionally or not) of what we will accept and what we will not stand for in a job. Is it pay? Is it culture and treatment of employees? Is it the type and quality of work? A combination of the above? And to what degree for each? Take some time to monitor yourself internally both before you jump into employment and as you experience things firsthand on the job, and come up with an *Ain't It* list for yourself. It's important to do this when you first start your career and revisit this list every 1–2 years after you begin working full time. When you actually dig your feet into a corporate setting and experience things like salary, annual bonus season, company culture, workforce diversity (or lack thereof), etc. firsthand, you may feel differently and prioritize differently than you initially thought you would.

If you begin to notice your current circumstances are violating your *Ain't It* list, try to identify the explicit aspects that are doing so and compare that against the tolerance threshold you've established for that value. If you have set a high tolerance threshold, maybe put a pin in it and revisit in a few months; continue to self-monitor your job satisfaction in the meantime to ensure it doesn't decline. If you have set a low tolerance threshold and your circumstances have significantly violated values on your *Ain't It* list, maybe it's time to brush up your resume. I can't have possibly thought through all scenarios in which someone may arrive at the conclusion that *their job ain't it*, but I wanted to provide you with a starter list of possible situations you may find yourself in, along with some words of affirmation and possible next steps when your *Ain't It* list is in the danger zone.

WHEN THE ROLE/DEPARTMENT AIN'T IT

Do you like your industry and company but dislike your current role? Depending on the organization, this may be the best situation of all the *"This Ain't Its"* to find yourself in. From my recruiting days, I realized quickly that it is nearly always more expensive to hire outside of the organization rather than retain existing talent. If your organization is smart, they will realize this too and be happy to promote hardworking individuals from within. If you're confident that your current employer *is it* but the role you're in *just ain't,* here are a few possible next steps you can take to start your journey of transferring internally to another role.

TALK TO YOUR MANAGER

You should feel comfortable letting your manager know what aspects of your role you love and want to do more of, as well as which aspects you don't care for and could do without. A good manager is going to create space for you to discuss this and will be genuinely interested in your response, as they want to do what they can to help you grow/develop in the areas you're most interested in pursuing for the remainder of your career. Whether you want to confide in your manager about what you like and what you don't, or take it a step further to tell them your mind is set on transferring out of the department entirely, you should definitely let them know what you're thinking sooner than later. You may be surprised how supportive they will be should you mention the possibility of transferring internally. They may even be willing to help you network internally and advocate for you to HR and/or the hiring manager

NETWORK INTERNALLY, ORGANICALLY

This is a great step to take if you have been considering transferring internally but are not quite yet certain you want to make a change. Networking is never a bad thing, and regardless of whether or not you act on the relationships you build immediately, knowing more individuals within your organization can only help you later on.

SEEK SPONSORSHIP

This may be the most natural step following your internal networking spree. If through networking you find an opening or team you are interested in, your next step (after consulting your current manager) should be seeking sponsorship from the hiring manager of the role or head of the department. Now, it is important to consider your organization's norms when seeking sponsorship. If you are a part of a relatively flat organization where outreach to department heads is encouraged, go for it. If you realize your organization doesn't quite do business that way, it may be best to go through channels such as your manager or the new role's hiring manager to seek sponsorship on your behalf.

START L&D ASAP

If you are interested in pivoting into a new role or field that requires skills outside of your portfolio, start your learning and development efforts ASAP. Even if you are not 100 percent certain you want to make the move, it will be highly beneficial for you to begin flirting with the skill sets and tools your new career path requires sooner than later. Interested in project management? Take an intro course. Want to explore more analytical facets of your current team? Seek out online resources to help enhance your Excel, SQL, or Tableau proficiency. These are just a few examples; you will know more than I what knowledge the specific path you are interested in requires.

Once you are aware of the knowledge gaps you have, start early trying to address them. The only way to really know if you want to try something new is to get involved more closely with the day-to-day of it, and watching YouTube videos, attending LinkedIn seminars, or registering for a free online course is a great way to confirm your hunch—not to mention your initiative will look great to your prospective new team or manager.

WHEN THE COMPANY AIN'T IT

Do you like your current industry and maybe even your current job, but can't stand to work for the specific company for a second longer? This section is tailored to you. Reasons one may arrive at this particular feeling of *This Ain't It* include but are not limited to their company. A company may get involved in scandals that make you uncomfortable, not celebrate diversity to the extent to which you'd like them to, experience a sharp shift in members of the management team, or consistently report bad revenue quarter over quarter, just to name a few examples. Whatever the reason may be, here are steps you can begin to take to help you feel like you are taking control of your destiny.

TALK TO YOUR FRIENDS

Compare experiences. Not only will this be cathartic by getting to vent you innermost layers of annoyance toward your employer, but you will also be able to benchmark whether or not there is a "better" gig out there. I put "better" in quotes because it is subjective. Better is in the eye of the beholder when it comes to new jobs. Preference varies from person to person and it all boils down to where a company satisfies (or doesn't) your list of values and the tolerance thresholds you set within them. Reference your values list when having these discussions with friends so you can be sure to cover all your bases when asking how their organizations compare to yours.

REACH OUT TO YOUR NETWORK

Do so in a tasteful way, of course. But let them know you're searching for alternatives. Put feelers out well before you begin your full-time search, because interview processes can often have a lengthy lifespan. Many of my friends would ask me for advice when they were going through application processes, whether for internships or full time, because of my background in recruiting. Having been on that side of the coin for a large portion of my career, what I say to everyone (even myself) applying for new roles is that the moment they submit an application for a role, they should set the expectation that they likely will *not* hear back from the company they just applied to. Sounds awful, right? That's not my intent; it's just the reality of most situations. I worked for a medium-sized company with little brand recognition and sometimes received nearly one thousand resumes for summer internship positions. Imagine how many resumes are submitted to the Googles and Facebooks of the world.

Assuming you're completely qualified for the job to which you are applying, getting your resume picked up is often the hardest part about landing a job. It often boils down to timing and a bit of luck. Leaning on your network when you're seeking a new position can be the small nudge you need in order to make it past that initial screen, especially when you're applying to larger organizations.

Your resume is a needle in a huge pile of needles, not a haystack, which makes it feel even more impossible to sift out. When you're flagged as an internal referral, your chances of getting your resume reviewed increase significantly. And should you make it through several rounds of interviews and receive an offer from this new organization, they have the reassurance that you are a proven entity, considering one of their employees endorsed you. Everyone wins!

WHEN THE PAY AIN'T IT

I'll start this one off by introducing two universal truths you should add to your catalog of important things to keep in mind:

1. Everyone feels underpaid.
2. Everyone wants more money.

That absolutely does not mean you shouldn't go for it during salary negotiations. I always encourage my friends to "ask for the extra five (thousand)." However, do keep this under your hat as a precautionary tale so you can manage your expectations for salary-related conversations appropriately.

In my experience, there are many things that may trigger one's dissatisfaction with their salary when they are new to the workforce. It could be anything from someone realizing they're actually grossly underpaid when compared to the market rate for their role, to someone chitchatting with their best friend during happy hour and finding out they make 10K less than their BFF. Either way, you are entitled to feeling you are undercompensated for the value that you provide to your firm, meaning you should feel empowered to ask for an increase during promotion/progression seasons. You can always ask; the reality is, however, you may not get what you want. Knowing all of this, if you begin to feel as if you deserve a pay bump, I recommend taking any or all of the following next steps.

CONSIDER YOUR TOTAL COMPENSATION PACKAGE

This is a big one for folks our age, especially if you are someone who has had the beautiful luxury of remaining on your parents' health insurance plan. What are your company's health care benefits? What is their 401(k) match? PTO plan? Beyond knowing what it is that your company offers in each of these facets, it's important to do some digging on Glassdoor or otherwise gauge what other companies out there are doing. Once you understand what benefits are considered standard for your industry and recognize where your company falls on the spectrum, you can factor this into your thought process. For instance, if your company has insanely awesome benefits, that may very well outweigh the extra 5K you want on your base salary.

DO YOUR RESEARCH—AND A LOT OF IT

Talking to friends who are in similar roles and industries is a great starting point for benchmarking where your salary stands. I think it's important to normalize knowledge by sharing salaries when the folks involved are mature enough to do so, because secrecy is a breeding ground for inequitable pay. However, talking to your close friends shouldn't be the extent of research that you do when benchmarking your salary against the market. Take advantage of job posting sites like Glassdoor, Indeed, LinkedIn, WayUp, etc. to triangulate an accurate salary range for roles similar to yours in the same industry.

Also understand that the Amazons, Facebooks, and Googles of

the world have the ability to pay more than nearly any other company that exists (so their data might need to be considered as outliers vs. standard). Reach out to your alma mater's career center to see what data they have on recent grad placements. Make sure you are rooting your market range in consistency, not anomalies!

TALK TO YOUR MANAGER

Just be straight up. Your manager is likely aware of the two universal truths we reviewed earlier, and probably relates to them as well. Ask for feedback on your current level of responsibilities and output. Follow that up with how you can best position yourself for a comp increase during mid-year or EOY reviews. Leverage your recurring touchpoints to have this conversation *ahead* of review season so you can pose these questions early, take note of their response, and document how you nailed everything they asked for (and then some, you overachiever!)

SEEK A COMPETING OFFER

Sometimes, the organization just doesn't have the means to meet your salary needs. Or perhaps the compensation team's hands are tied by weird rules and red tape the organization has set regarding comp bands. Whatever the reason may be, you have to consider your tolerance threshold. If you are adamant about receiving an increase, sometimes a live job offer is a good way to demonstrate your value and require your firm to act quickly. Just know there is always the risk that your company does not respond the way you'd hope and tells you to "have fun and enjoy the new role." But perhaps that is a risk worth taking, depending on how over things you are.

20.
THE JIG IS UP

I am of the mind that the antithesis of *"This Ain't It"* is *"The Jig Is Up."*

That's right. This chapter is for those on the completely opposite end of the spectrum regarding significant job or organizational changes. It's for those who are completely content and fulfilled in their current role but, due to circumstances outside of their control, are forced into a new position, reporting line, and/or department that is entirely different than the job that they have grown to love. These types of changes can come in a variety of packages. They could be things that are slightly bothersome but that you easily adapt to, or they might be earth-shattering and have you seriously asking yourself, *Is this worth staying for?* This chapter focuses on the types of changes described by the latter response.

While the output of both *"This Ain't It"* and *"The Jig Is Up"* conclusions are the same (they likely result in a change of your job title, department, organization, or a combination of the three), it felt important to separate the two because they look and feel completely different. *"This Ain't It"* is empowering. It is a tale of grabbing life and your current circumstances by the balls and creating your own destiny. It is a beautiful story of realizing your dreams and capabilities and putting them into motion. *"The Jig Is Up"* is a significantly sadder narrative. In this story, it feels like your circumstances are grabbing *you* by the balls and forcing you into change that you didn't ask for. It is a tale of feeling that your time working your dream job, with your dream team, and/or reporting to your dream manager was short-lived; gone too soon with nothing you can do to bring it back.

When you initially realize *The Jig Is Up*, you may be in a bit of denial. A very common reaction to change is to cling to aspects of your surroundings that remain the same, as they are the only pieces of ground you feel are not moving out from under your feet. This might be your manager should your organization be acquired and absorbed into a new parent company. This may be your team should your manager suddenly resign or be let go. I encourage you to speak thoughtfully but freely with whoever is your "safe ground" during tumultuous times at work. As we've discussed in previous chapters, just like you are a human being with fears and emotions, so are your colleagues. If you are feeling a certain way about recent changes your organization has experienced, it is likely that many others feel similarly. So find them, and talk to them. There is power in vulnerability, and power in numbers.

When I initially experienced some of the Potential Causes of Why the Jig is Up, I realized that part of the reason I reacted so sensitively to each scenario is because I was new to each one. It was a series of firsts; unfortunately, a slightly more brutal parade of "firsts" than I would have preferred. So if and as you experience any of the below, be prepared that you (understandably so) may react emotionally, and nothing is wrong with that. When you do, remind yourself that the reason you seem far more impacted by this than some of your more senior colleagues may be because this is new for you. It's the first time that your corporate enthusiasm and innocence is shattered. Whereas theirs has probably been broken in for quite some time now.

POTENTIAL CAUSES OF WHY THE JIG IS UP

More things can occur than you may realize that can cause shifts in your immediate working environment. The jury is still out on which suck worse, because they all suck pretty bad.

RESIGNATIONS

It's always bittersweet when someone you care about or enjoy working within the organization resigns. Sweet because you are happy for them and whatever the next step in their career is. Bitter because they're leaving you behind to deal with all the work madness you used to face together (and find their replacement). What makes the resignation the most interesting is *why* someone decided to resign. Sometimes it's things that are totally expected and/or out of anyone's control: the individual wants to relocate, they've been at the company for a significant stretch of time and it's due time for something new, or they stumbled upon an incredible opportunity elsewhere that they absolutely couldn't turn down. When their rationale seems a little less standard, it's these instances you want to pay close attention to. Did they resign because the company's performance is tanking? Because the new wave of leadership is a mess? Something different but equally as concerning? If any of these are the case, maybe it's a sign you should do a bit more digging and see if anyone else around you is contemplating jumping ship.

LAYOFFS

Ah, layoffs—resignation's ugly twin sibling. The ends are the same, but the means are much harder to swallow. It sounds ridiculous but layoffs are much more common than I expected coming into the corporate world. Perhaps part of the reason I was so naive to the fact that many individuals get let go from their jobs each year is the fact that I never witnessed anyone close to me (a parent, friend's parent, or friend) go through this. Layoffs are very difficult to swallow, because no matter what the rationale behind the decision to let folks go, it's never easy to watch someone's source of stability and income get ripped out from under them.

REORGS

A reorg (aka reorganization) is sometimes good, sometimes shit. Regardless, I can almost guarantee that whenever significant changes occur within your organization, the individuals who are directly impacted may initially act with reservation. Understandably so, as anything that rocks the boat can cause skepticism. The worse of a job the company does at communicating the organizational change, the more likely it is that employees raise an eyebrow at the move.

Reasons for major organizational changes can be all across the board: a group is underperforming and needs different/closer supervision, the organization has outgrown its flat hierarchical structure and needs to change the way it operates, repositioning of key teams may further increase efficiency and enable scalability, a department is being underutilized and would benefit from reporting into a subject matter expert rather than a business head, etc. This is a more logical list of reasons organizational changes occur. A *less* logical lists of reasons exists, and they are often political in nature. You'll be surprised to see how many companies are saturated in politics. Taking teams away from certain leaders and reassigning them to others can be nothing more than a power move, or preparation for a senior leader to be let go a few months down the line.

Because of the multiple possibilities behind why reorgs can occur, they might seem malicious in nature to start, but surprisingly people are often quite satisfied with organizational changes after the benefits are recognizable. Really, time is the only way to tell if you feel the changes that have been made are positive. Because of this, I encourage you to remain skeptical (of course, prepare and protect yourself) but also keep an open mind. Not all reorgs are bad.

ACQUISITIONS

The best way to describe an acquisition is a reorg on steroids. No two acquisitions will look the same. And just like reorgs, you might really like the new parent company and the way their investment/capabilities allow your teams to achieve their goals much more quickly than you could have as a single entity. Or you might be totally infiltrated by the new parent company, everything you once knew of your company may disappear, and product lines are canceled, leading to layoffs.

Just like with reorgs, only time will tell. Acquisitions are (in my opinion) the most turbulent of all of the reasons I've listed out so far; the main reason being that they more often than not end up being reorgs, layoffs, *and* resignations all wrapped into one event.

MUCH WORSE

Yeah, it can always get worse, believe it or not. There is a whole lot of ugly to be seen in the corporate world. If the people who are hired to keep these things hidden and wrapped in a tidy bow are excelling in their roles, you may never realize exactly how ugly things can get. That's probably for the best. But if things slip through the cracks or get blasted in a *New York Times* article, you might hear about it, your new hire naivety will be ruined, your opinion of your organization and perhaps people in it may change, and you might find yourself in a moral conflict. This *Much Worse* category can span across things such as embezzlement, sexual harassment lawsuits, exploiting immigrant employees, wrongful discrimination, etc. Any awful headline you've seen previously or case study you've analyzed in college is fair game in terms of mistakes your employer can make.

What do you do when they make them? I don't think there is any right or wrong answer. Whether you speak up and voice your disappointment and anger, resign, or elect to take no action, you are within your rights. It's significantly easier said than done to outright tell the machine that signs your paycheck that they've royally fucked up and you think incredibly low of them for doing so. I can see why people may hesitate to do that. But feel empowered to have those conversations (probably a bit more polished than how I just framed it) if you need to do so in order to ease your conscience while working there. Be comfortable making it clear to fellow colleagues and external stakeholders you may interact with that you do not identify or agree with the decisions made by your company. And then ask yourself: *is this truly the place I want to be?*

THE NEWS IS OUT—REACTING AND ACTING

Let's fast-forward a bit. After you realize *The Jig Is Up* and *The News Is Out* (the band Styx, anybody?), where do you go next? How might you feel, and therefore react, when faced with one or many of the above reasons behind the jig? Let's use a few hypotheticals to illustrate what might run through your mind.

Juan's firm got acquired 18 months into his first role. He didn't much care about the firm getting acquired at first because employees were not given any detailed direction at the time the announcement was made. Therefore he had no reason at the time to believe that anything was going to change significantly in the short term. The acquisition was more of an intangible object—something he heard about, discussed often with colleagues, and realized was running in the background of his day-to-day. But because he wasn't directly involved with merger-related conversations and hadn't met anyone from the parent company yet, the first month or so was fine. Business as usual. Until it wasn't.

When the changes started coming, they didn't seem to stop. Juan soon found himself in the face of a dumpster fire of changes he wasn't thrilled about. People who contributed to his job satisfaction were either reorged out of reach, laid off, or chose to resign. His reporting line changed and he was segregated from the remaining members of the team of he once played an integral part. The acquisition was no longer an enigma; it was now *very* fucking tangible.

Juan is young, single, and probably pours more of himself into his work than is good for anyone involved. He's not currently dating a human being, so he essentially filled that void of his life by dating his work. Just over a year later, the job and company he envisioned his near-term future with suddenly vanished with little notice in advance. He kind of felt like his ass got broken up with. No, he *definitely* felt like his ass got broken up with (and was more upset about this breakup than the last time he got dumped). Very emotional about the changes that took place, Juan began looking for a new job.

Pivoting to *layoffs*, a Profreshional named Ani witnessed her dear friend getting fired only 2 months into her first full-time gig. She was angry beyond what one would consider mature or appropriate for an office setting. So angry that her fury manifested as tears as she sat fuming at her desk. Just two weeks later, a story was leaked and *Much Worse* unveiled itself to the employees of her firm. Ani didn't know what to do. She struggled very much with an internal dilemma of whether or not she should take action after the events unfolded; she felt she should do more to demonstrate her disgust (like look for a new job). But only two months into her career and on the horizon of a fast-track to a promotion, she didn't want to pack her bags just yet. She was concerned that made her a bad friend to the employees personally impacted by *Layoffs*. She feared that made her a poor advocate for the types of organizations that would disagree with the *Much Worse* events that occurred.

I give you these two example scenarios to show how differently you and others may react when *The Jig Is Up*. It may not be realistic to resign and find a new job every time an unwanted and unexpected change takes place in your firm. Or maybe it is, if the events are spaced out enough and if they violate your personal values and boundaries enough to push you to that point.

***

Humans are creatures of habit. Especially when it comes to habits that directly influence one's feelings of safety, stability, and security. No matter how spontaneous we may proclaim to be, no matter how happy we are to wing it when it comes to our vacation plans, when a similar level of ambiguity and randomness is applied to a work setting, it is infinitely more unsettling. Why is that? It's because work is a place, a thing, that we expect to remain (relatively) constant. We as humans crave stability in our jobs, because this guarantees stability for some of our most basic needs as people: food, shelter, water, and sociability. When changes occur that are outside of our internal tolerance thresholds, or are drastic in nature (such as layoffs, unexpected resignations from key talent or leadership, or lawsuits), we do not respond well. And rightfully so. When our work environment is threatened, we feel that our most basic needs as humans are being threatened too. It is perfectly normal and acceptable for you to be anxious, pissed off, or just plain sad when changes within your organization occur. (Notice I say *when* and not *if*, because if I've learned anything in my first few years of employment, change will for damn sure happen and once it gets started it often doesn't stop).

There is no right or wrong way to respond when shifts occur. If your fear of looking for another job overpowers your disgust for the way your organization has handled a certain event, that is okay. I understand and support you. If you don't care to stick around post-acquisition to see if any of these "good opportunities" are a fit for you, that's a totally valid conclusion too. You are empowered to make that choice. I understand you and support you.

I hope by this point you've begun to piece together that there is no "right" or "wrong" way to design the first few years of your career. That doesn't mean there aren't very obvious "rights" or wins, and very obvious "wrongs" or fuckups (you should steer clear of these). But when it comes down to what you like, don't like, what upsets you and what you can't be bothered to care about, it will vary from person to person. It is both terrifying and exhilarating knowing that you are totally and completely in the driver's seat here. For years and years to come. You don't have to play by anyone's rules, really. At any point in time you can decide enough of something is enough, and reopen your job search.

Approach these decisions with an open mind, with as objective of a view as possible. Entertain the devil's advocate, and lean on friends, family members, or colleagues you deeply trust for advice or affirmation. But at the end of the day, only you know how you feel. Only you are in touch with your goals and what it will take to experience your deepest feelings of fulfillment. You need to trust *yourself*. And as much as it sucks, when the *jig is up*, it may just be time to accept it and pivot accordingly.

21.
YOU ARE YOUR MENTORS

The first few years of your career are going to fly by. I know I sound like your grandmother by saying that, but it's undeniably true. Here I am, three years in, feeling like I've aged nearly ten, yet at the same time it seems impossible that any time has passed at all. Time seems to move at an accelerated pace during these first few years because you're constantly over-stimulated; you are learning by experience across a wide variety of subject matters.

Personal life. Work. Living with roommates. Living on your own. Self-actualization. Who you are. Who you want to be. What you want from life. Maintaining old friendships. Finding new friendships. Excitement of dating in a new city. Disappointment of dating in a new city. Trying to navigate these subjects are difficult enough as is, much less trying to do so within the confines of a 40- 50-hour workweek.

Reflection is important, critically so during these first few years of your adult life. Just like how your freshman year of college or high school was likely full of beauty, heartbreak, magic, foolishness, ugliness, stress, wins, losses, and everything in between, so will the freshman term of your professional life. You'll reflect back in a few years' time and think, *Wow, look how much I have learned; look how tall I've grown.*

Keeping a paper trail of your first few years in the corporate world (whether shorthand notes here or there, or significantly detailed journal entries) will be a good time capsule for you to revisit. Writing out events as they unfold, how you reacted to them, strategies that led to big triumphs, or approaches that resulted in failure, will help you begin to nail down your own theories about best practices. Having observations to refer back to will play a key role in helping you establish and refine your professional brand, identify your unique competitive advantage in the workforce, and coin your own set of mantras that have helped you achieve success. And who knows, in three years you might summarize all of *your* learnings into a book that turns out infinitely better than mine!

But as important as it is to reflect on and document how we're growing and changing and what we're learning, it is even more important to recognize and document that we are not making these strides on our own.

I once heard in a TED Talk that no newly released songs are actually new. For generations, all songs that are created pull in some aspect of existing rhythms or musical patterns. A similar concept yet different application I've read is that human beings are a combination of the five individuals they spend the majority of their time with. This theory of previous experiences impacting what we produce and who we are (whether consciously or subconsciously) is applicable to every facet of our lives, professional included.

I firmly believe that who we are as professionals is directly attributed to the people who have invested in us early on, the projects and challenges we were exposed to, and the other professionals we've had the chance to collaborate with. Any mantra we think we develop is not an entirely new epiphany. Our ways of working are not revolutionary to the universe. A version of what we live by and how we guide our work habits has likely existed before, and was passed on to us through interactions with others. The mantras and habits that make up the core of our professional brands and successes are a product of exposure. It is all thanks to the people we've crossed paths with who want us to succeed. I boil this theory down into the last and final mantra I want to leave you all with: *You are your mentors.*

This isn't me trying to shit on your parade of how awesome you are and how hard you work; you absolutely can still attribute *your* success to *you.* But you cannot do so entirely in the absence of also thanking others who have helped shape you. When we begin our corporate journey, we are the clay, we are not the artist. We need a little bit of help shaping our habits and skills, otherwise three years down the road we end up still looking like just a blob of dough. Because we are highly impressionable when we first begin our corporate journey, it is all the more important to identify and cling to good people and good mentors. Over time we become a compilation of all the best parts of everyone who has taken the time out of their life to teach us something. For that, we should show them an immense amount of gratitude.

People aren't paid to give a shit about the new kid. Sure, it is in a team's best interest to invest in their junior talent because it in turn helps them build their internal pipeline for future management prospects. But to find someone who cares beyond training you to deliver quality output, and beyond the ROI they will get from teaching you, is rare. Coming across someone who consistently takes time out of their already stretched day to *really care about you*—asking how you're adjusting both inside and outside of the workplace, encouraging you to put your health first, acting as a confidant, and telling you when you're being too hard on yourself and need a break—is *extremely rare*. So if you find yourselves crossing paths with someone like that, make sure you thoroughly appreciate them, celebrate them by giving them the credit they deserve, and stay close to them.

FINDING GOOD MENTORS

Identifying and building rapport with good mentors is often much easier said than done. Especially in today's age of remote work and onboarding, having limited in-person collaboration might make it incredibly challenging to organically build mentor-mentee relationships. If you're not sure where to start identifying and engaging mentor prospects, this next section details all the tips and tricks that have helped me work some mentor magic in the past.

YOU BRING IN WHAT YOU PUT OUT

If you are genuinely eager to learn best practices quickly and make an impact in your role and on your organization, that will come through in your interactions with people. If you are seeking out certain individuals solely because you think building a good rapport with them will help them elevate your career, that will come through in your interactions too. Most people have enough EQ to decipher who is well-intended in their outreach for mentorship and who is trying to climb the social ladder. If you put out energy and intention closer to the former, those are the types of individuals you will find yourself surrounded by. You'll be far more likely to establish a genuine relationship. If you put out energy and intention closer to the latter, you will likely turn people off from wanting to help you, as they will see very early on that you're interacting with them solely because you think you'll score a big gain.

If trying to climb the corporate ladder as quickly as possible with little to no regard for the people you step on in the process is your angle, it may work for a bit, but your "wins" will eventually hit a ceiling. This ties in nicely with my next point.

SEE PEOPLE AS PEOPLE

I had the unique privilege of working in a relatively flat organization, meaning that people of all levels were very accessible to anyone and everyone across the firm. Our CEO knew me by name and would send a wave as I passed by him in the common areas. That isn't because I was super awesome or popular or an entry-level prodigy; it was just the culture of our firm. And while he wanted to be recognized and respected internally as the CEO of our company, he also wanted to be recognized and respected by employees as a human being. I think most people feel this way regardless of the level their job title is.

Think about how you want to be perceived by your colleagues when you walk into a meeting room. Do you want them to see you as a "junior" analyst? Only see you as your age? Believe your capabilities are limited just because you're an entry-level hire? Of course not. You want to walk into that meeting room and be greeted as a fellow peer. A human being.

Assumptions about your age or title aside, senior leadership may feel similarly when walking into an afternoon happy hour. You should absolutely display your respect for them and their status when preparing for 1:1 conversations, or when addressing them via written communications. However, do not let your awareness of their title overwhelm your perception and treatment of them as human beings. Do not assume that mid-level management and senior leaders of an organization value trust and comradery any less than colleagues

205

you interact with at the lower levels of an org chart. By seeing mid-to senior-level managers as people, asking them how *they* are doing, inquiring (within a respectable boundary) about their family or hobbies, you may just make their day enough to plant a seed for further rapport-building and possible mentorship.

UNDERSTAND MENTORSHIP VS. SPONSORSHIP

Understanding what you should expect from a mentor is key in identifying a good candidate. I think of mentorship as tequila and sponsorship as mezcal: not all mentors can sponsor, but all sponsors can mentor. Mentors might be within 2 or 3 years of your tenure. Sponsors are likely much more senior. Sponsors will have the clout and ability to influence decisions and put your name in the hat for key projects, promotions, etc. Mentors may or may not be able to do that for you. However, mentors can help you with a much wider array of situations and issues, talking you through topics that may not even directly have to do with work.

LEAD THE CHARGE

It's not that people aren't willing to take the time out of their day to chat; it's just that they get so caught up in their day-to-day that they may forget to reach out first. So take that burden from them and lead the charge. Schedule your monthly recurring meeting. Continue to check in intermittently to remain relevant.

GIVE IT TIME

Even when you attend formal networking events or participate in a formal mentorship program, it may take a few sessions to establish a good rapport. It's almost like finding a therapist; you need to let them get to know you over a few sessions before you can come to the conclusion as to whether or not they're the one for you.

KEEPING GOOD MENTORS

Finding mentors is the first step, but the work does not stop there. Like any relationship in life, you have to continuously invest in the relationships you build with your mentors or else they will eventually taper off. Odds are other people look at the same awesome individuals you do to build mentor-mentee relationships. If you want to ensure you continue to have a seat at your mentor's mentee table, here are a few strategies you can apply.

THANK THEM FREQUENTLY

Let them know the impact they've made. You'd be surprised at how little people are thanked for their work.

HYPE THEM UP TO THEIR PEERS AND SENIOR LEADERSHIP

Find ways to incorporate your gratitude for them in conversations you have with other leaders in the organization. Be sure to give them credit for what they've taught or assisted you with while you're presenting during a meeting. Now, not all of the people you've internalized a lesson from will be invested in aspects of your personal life. You will have mentors of varying degrees of intensity and intimacy, which is completely OK because variety is the spice of life. Make sure to keep track of who these key people are, what role they have played in your development, and what you've learned from them, and adjust how often you keep up with them accordingly.

BRING SOMETHING TO THE TABLE TOO

Your mind may jump to the conclusion that there is no possible way you can provide anything to your mentors in return, because the whole point of having one is that *they* teach *you* things. That is true to a degree, but it doesn't necessarily mean you can't bring anything to the table to ensure that your relationship is mutually beneficial. If you aren't confident that you can bring them grand life lessons and how-tos for certain tools or technologies, bring them youthful optimism and energy. Bring them support. Ask them how they're doing in return, and listen. Bring them your perspective. They might appreciate how you see things differently from them/their generation.

* * *

Like anything in life, good things come to those who wait—strong mentorship and professional relationships included. Do not be discouraged if you don't seem to stumble across the perfect mentor/mentee dynamic within your first week of working. Continue to reach out to subject matter experts across your organization, sharing your enthusiasm for learning and establishing a strong rapport. Also keep in mind that these types of relationship comes in a variety of intensity and longevity. You might be given the best nuggets of advice from someone you briefly cross paths with and don't consider to be a long-term mentor at all. Or you might learn something new from someone below or beside you in your organization, not fitting the "traditional mold" for mentorship. Regardless of what your mentor dynamics turn out to be and when they end up appearing, it will be beneficial for you to include who taught you what lessons as you document how your first few years of corporate life unfold.

This book is *my* journal of how the past few years of adjusting to corporate environments and adulthood unfolded. My Profreshional

Year included the magic of moving to New York City, majorly fucking up on projects, learning by fire, drunk nights and next-day hangovers with colleagues, self-work and self-forgiveness, a total change in my career path, and an incredible fleet of mentors who have poured into me beyond what I could ever possibly deserve or repay. But in the spirit of *You Are Your Mentors*, I at least had to try. This book is my attempt to repay those who have helped shape me into the young professional I am today.

PART THREE

FROM THE MASSES

I recognize the potential reach and applicability of this book is limited, given that the stories and corresponding words of advice throughout are told from only my perspective. I know that how I perceive and analyze the world may differ from the way that you do since we are unique in our experiences, strengths, and even career paths. In an attempt to try to combat any dissonance, I have asked some of the most cherished and well-respected members of my network to share their own experiences and insights.

Each of my dear friends and colleagues listed below are what I call Profreshional Alumni because they have recently experienced their own Profreshional Year and have lived to tell the tale—just like you will (or already have)! The directory contains a brief bio of who they are, including how their identities impact their experience of the working world, their current job title and industry, and a page number guiding you to their insightful message.

Happy reading!

DIRECTORY OF PROFRESHIONAL ALUMNI

THEIR MESSAGES TO YOU

FROM MICHELLE I:

Michelle is a Nigerian-American woman and behavioral health startup founder. She obtained a bachelor's degree in marketing with a concentration in math and media.

She is currently working in consumer technology as a product manager at Boston Consulting Group.

"Create a networking strategy. When you enter the workforce you will be surrounded by brilliant people. Brilliance comes in a plethora of shades: experience, exposure, and connections, all of which give you perspective. As an early professional, the more experience and exposure you can get, the more seasoned your perspective becomes. The question is, where do you start and how can you make an impact?

How to Start:
- Start small and within your direct team (e.g., manager, colleague, etc.), then ask them who they recommend you reach out to.
- A few sample reasons behind your outreach: to understand

more about marketing, to hear more about data analytics, to gain perspective on the company culture, or just in general!

How to Make an Impact:

- There is plenty of advice on questions to ask, but not enough on how to create a conversation that flows. Coffee chats are one good way of connecting with new people versus merely adding someone to your network.
- Think about coffee chats like this: in about two years, you will be on the other side of the table with an early professional asking you similar questions. How would you like it to go? What questions would you be excited to answer?

Loosen up, show your personality, and remember that the core of community building is taking a genuine interest in the lives of others. The context of the conversation will start to fade after a while, but the feeling a person gets when they feel listened to will remain.

I've come across a very diverse set of people: startup founders, past actresses/models, gardeners, wine connoisseurs, and active investors. Go out on a limb and set up the coffee chats, especially when you're new, because most people are excited to welcome you in! If for nothing else, at least a few people you work with will have a fascinating story to tell.

Disclaimer: There will be many people you want to meet, but as your workload starts to increase, you may find less time to network. Find ways to prioritize it anyway. You'll do great."

FROM MARQEE I:

Marqee is proud to be a Black male and licensed CPA. He obtained a bachelor's and master's in accounting from the University of Georgia.

He is currently working in accounting as a senior tax associate at PricewaterhouseCoopers LLP.

Poet William E. Henley's "*I am the master of my fate: I am the captain of my soul*" is the mantra that guided my life in college, but I did not realize the power of that statement until I started to work full time. Going into any job field, not just corporate America, if you do not truly know yourself or have confidence in your story, someone else will create one for you. That story will then mold your brand and your peers' perception of you. *Do not let that happen.*

Your career is what *you* make it, not someone sitting in the cubicle beside you. And yes, you may just be starting your career, and not really sure of your purpose or what your brand is. But that is the beauty in the word "your"—it's up to *you* to decide. Your purpose and brand may not be the same as when you first began your career. It molds with you; it grows. So make sure you're the one cultivating it and giving it life because *you* are the master of your fate. *You* are the captain of your soul.

———

FROM WILLIAM K:

William is an Atlanta native and holds a bachelor's degree in marketing.

He is currently self-employed, working in branding/marketing as a freelance branding/ design consultant.

"Focus fiercely and exclusively on your own path. It is very easy, especially in the first couple of years out of college, to look at the paths of your peers and compare them to your own. A great example of this is when everyone is landing their first jobs at different places. Culturally, certain employers are considered more "impressive" names than others. Value is also placed on getting a job as quickly as possible, even before graduation. Do not get caught up in this. Your path is yours to own, control, and make the most of. There are different yet equal opportunities in every venture in life. Focus on maximizing yours.

P.S. This is helpful for all areas of life, not just professionally."

––––––

FROM JOSH C:

Josh is a Georgia native and self-identifies as a "Band Kid." He holds a bachelor's degree in geography and comparative literature with a certificate in GIS (Geographic Information Systems).

He currently works in software/ technology as a product writer at Esri.

"Everything is going to feel like it's urgent, and that should come as no surprise since we're conditioned to think that way. In high school we're told to join as many organizations as possible, spend every waking moment building our GPA, find a good school, etc. In college it's more of the same, except we're told that it's not our academic career that's at stake, but our entire life. Then you graduate and find what you've supposedly been working toward for the past decade and . . . now what?

School, work, and life are all too often seen as a ladder to climb, and when the next rung is missing, our reach can falter. This was how I felt several months after graduating college. My advice to you is not to stop climbing, or striving to find the next best thing for yourself, but rather widen your perspective to what that can look like. Rather than planning for the years ahead, as you have been up to this moment, allow yourself to find success and fulfillment in the everydayness. Focus on what's in front of you. Focus on being the very best at whatever task you're given, no matter how mundane it may be. Be vocal and let your peers know you have something to offer, no matter how junior you may be. As Cal Newport says, *"Be so good they can't ignore you."*

Be right where you are, at least for now. Glance at the horizon every so often, but grant yourself the serenity of finding motivation in what's right in front of you. Lean on your friends and your chosen family. Take a deep breath. The urgency will subside."

———

FROM MATT B:

Matt self-identifies as a Georgia native, Asian-American, and LGBTQ. He holds a bachelor's degree in social work, and he is a master's of nonprofit management student and a former teacher.

He currently works in education as a leadership development specialist (coach for new teachers) at Teach for America.

"Know your goals. Where do you see yourself in the next year, five years, ten years? Once you know your goals, make a plan. Along the way, make sure you are checking off a small part of your plan, and you will be great!

At the same time, don't forget to take care of yourself. No one knows your needs better than you. Be intentional about prioritizing your wellness (social, emotional, physical), and don't be afraid to meet your needs before helping others. We need you for the long haul."

FROM DOUGLAS D:

Douglas self-identifies as a gay male and is a Troy University summa cum laude grad.

He currently works in insurance as a commercial insurance claims specialist at Sompo International.

"One thing I've learned in my short tenure working in corporate America: You WILL Fail. How we respond to failure, however, is what makes or breaks us in the professional world. My advice: don't let failure derail you. One thing I've found most helpful in my career, especially as a corporate trainee, is to free myself up from the expectations of perfection. That way, when mistakes ensue, they can be embraced. When we embrace our shortcomings, we're able to learn, develop, and ultimately flourish.

I think one key to success, whether you're crushing it or barely surviving, is to stay humble. Posturing yourself in humility will set you apart from your peers. Your managers and mentors *want* to teach and develop you, but it's quite challenging to develop an individual who presents themselves as though they already possess the knowledge or insight. There's a lot of beauty in being able to acknowledge that you don't know everything. Additionally, when we posture ourselves in humility, the inevitable failures and mistakes will sting far less."

_____

FROM VALENTINA P:

Valentina is a female and DACA recipient. She holds a bachelor's degree in communications.

She currently works in digital media as a digital media consultant at SUNFLOWERVALENTINE.

"My advice to young professionals comes from a point of empathy and open kindness. I urge open minds and the capability to listen to be at the forefront of any career you embark on. There will be moments of self-doubt, as well as opportunities that do not pan out the way you expect. These instances will shape, mold, and prepare you for the growth you will least expect within your life."

_____

FROM SARAH R:

Sarah identifies as a woman and an advocate. She holds a bachelor's degree in social work as well as a Juris Doctor.

She currently works in public interest (legal) as an assistant public defender at Georgia Public Defender Council.

"Like many other new professionals, I strive to impress my superiors and surpass each and every expectation. A year in, I still struggle with the imposter syndrome that comes with growing in a new position. The pervasive thoughts sound a lot like, *If another attorney were assigned this case, they would do a better job for this client than I can.* Thoughts like those have shut me down completely for the entirety of an afternoon if I let them. They make me question each and every thing I do, and make me feel as though no matter how much time and energy I expend, I won't be good enough to do the work. None of which is true. In fact, I work very hard for my clients.

I have done things on cases that other, more seasoned attorneys would not have taken the time to do. I have helped people. And that's what keeps me going every day. Those thoughts cannot disarm me; they have to drive me to keep learning, keep asking questions, and keep fighting for justice for my clients. I have the absolute privilege to advocate for indigent criminal defendants, and I am never going to be "perfect" at this beautiful, messy (oftentimes thankless) work. Shifting my mindset and holding those intrusive thoughts captive when I feel myself starting to sink into myself has forever changed the game.

I hope that anyone who steps into a new career knows that they were chosen to do hard things, and they are capable of doing them. But in order to be effective, we have to show ourselves grace, take much-needed breaks, and for the love of all that is holy, ask for help when we need it. In sum, we can be in a constant state of growth and still be perfectly equipped for the job. We just need to know where and how to access the resources to help us get to that next step of greatness. Don't quit when it gets hard, and remember to love on yourselves the way you would love on your best friend starting their new job. You're going to do amazing things!"

———

FROM NICOLE B:

Nicole identifies as a Black woman and Georgia native. She is a graduate of the University of Georgia and holds a bachelor's degree in advertising.

She currently works in marketing/social media as a content strategist at The Modern Green Book.

"The transition from my academic to professional career was (and still is) interesting given that it took place in the middle of the COVID-19 pandemic. I graduated in May 2020 and many (and by many, I mean all) of my plans were derailed. It was a really rough time for me personally, and I dissociated from a lot of my professional endeavors. I moved back in with my parents with no job offers, I lost a lot of my communication skills, and the anxiety I felt about interviewing became almost unbearable. It ultimately made me look to new ways to start my career and to provide services in general.

For me, it was through a family friend that I found an opportunity to start freelance advertising and social media marketing. It is a year later, and I have yet to find that full-time position, but I am working with all kinds of businesses and agencies until I find an opportunity that suits me. The best token of advice I can give is to be fluid and open to opportunities and positions that you may not have considered. If you aren't raking in offers and interview callbacks out of the gate, first of all, don't worry, give yourself grace and time (I certainly did), consider other options, get creative, and you will settle into a groove and ultimately a position that's right for you."

———

FROM ANDREA V:

Andrea studied engineering at the Georgia Institute of Technology. She feels that studying engineering gave her the confidence and work ethic she needed to pursue any career.

She currently works in high school education as the director of academic and college counseling at Holy Spirit Preparatory.

"Take advantage of being the new face in the office. Similarly to your freshman year of college, say yes to every single social opportunity for the first year and participate wholeheartedly. Additionally, open yourself to the advice of others. You were not hired because you already know everything; you were hired because they trust your capacity to ask questions and learn the material. Recognize that your coworkers receive tremendous satisfaction from being able to share their knowledge and wisdom with you—and asking for 1:1 help or advice is one of the least intimidating ways to begin your workplace friendships."

FROM CHRIS O:

Chris uses he/him pronouns and is a Bronx native/Brooklyn transplant. He holds a bachelor's degree in neuroscience and is a proud Puerto Rican, brother, son, and friend.

He currently works in staffing/DEIB/technology as a senior customer success specialist at Jopwell.

"I have two pieces of advice for those who are entering the workforce.

The first being that you seek out an environment in which you feel comfortable and confident growing. It's easy to go for the first opportunity that falls in your lap (and I completely understand every circumstance is different, especially for low-income and underrepresented people/groups), but if you have the liberty and privilege to find a space where you feel seen, then do it because a seed in bad soil struggles to grow.

The second piece of advice, and pardon the sports analogy, would be to box above your weight class. For some it may be daunting to walk into a new environment, and for that reason it is easy to take a back seat as you absorb information. Definitely be inquisitive and challenge convention. If you feel like a process doesn't make sense during your first week, challenge it. At the very least you'll learn why the process works the way it does, or you'll immediately make yourself stand out by identifying an area of improvement."

———

FROM CHRIS M:

Chris identifies as a Black male, Georgia native, and college graduate.

He currently works within the tech industry in product partnerships at Squarespace.

"One piece of advice I would like to share with young professionals is to be mindful of the impact your first manager can have on the trajectory of your career. When I first joined the workforce two years ago, I was very lucky to have a manager who believed in putting her team members in positions to win. As a result, my first role out of college allowed me to manage partnerships with Samsung Pay and Google Pay, launch money movement products for a global bank, and take on other high visibility projects at the firm. None of these opportunities would have been possible without my manager trusting my ability to do great work.

During the process of transitioning to a new role, many hiring managers and recruiters were impressed with the depth of my experience at such an early point in my career. Navigating this process highlighted the importance of making sure your manager is invested in your growth and professional development. When choosing your first role out of college, it's important to use the recruiting process to learn more about your manager and then the investment they make in their people."

FINAL NOTE

Unfortunately, our time together has come to an end. First and foremost, I want to thank you so much for coming along for this ride. What I want to leave you with is confidence and excitement. You clearly want to succeed in life and in your career because you are here, trying to learn and better prepare yourself for what may lie ahead. The Profreshional Year is one of the biggest, yet best, clusterfucks of a year life has to offer. It is thrilling, exhausting, and a hell of a lot of hard work. But I know you will excel through it and I cannot wait to see the impact you make in your organizations and the world around us.

Remember, you are not alone. In fact, you are very much surrounded by people who may think, feel, and fear the same exact things you do. Believe with conviction that you are capable of becoming all of the things that you aspire to be. Your Profreshional Year and longer-term career will be better for it.

ACKNOWLEDGMENTS

I chewed on the idea of *Profreshional* for nearly two years before finding the courage to take to the keyboard and seriously try writing this thing. Several people championed the idea from the start and have cheered me on through every step of the writing and publishing process. To each of you, thank you. This book would not exist without you.

To my editors Patrick Price and Brooks Becker, thank you for making my raw inputs sparkle. This book would not exist without you.

To the several individuals who participated in beta reading sessions and contributed brutally honest feedback, thank you. This book would not exist without you.

To the group of talented young professionals who were willing to share their stories in Part Three: From the Masses, thank you. This book would not exist without you.

To Mahroo Sameen, who brought my cover art vision and interior charts to life with brilliant, vibrant graphic designs, thank you. This book would not exist without you.

To Svyatoslav Sudakov who answered my cry for help on Reddit and created the initial interior formatting, thank you. This book would not exist without you.

To Jack Samuels, who assisted with my every business/waiver-related need without hesitation, thank you. This book would not exist without you.

To Diann Melo, whose advice unknowingly inspired "Get a Hobby, Hunny," thank you. This book would not exist without you.

To Nick McEwen, for your knowledge-sharing of the *Tiny Red Box Trick* and many other technical project management skills, thank you. This book would not exist without you.

To the Quant, BI, NLP, and Structured Data Science Teams who took a chance on my capabilities and gave me a job to sorely miss, thank you. This book would not exist without you.

Lastly, to the list of people who have impacted me beyond what the blurbs I've written below can capture, thank you. This book would not exist without you.

———

Maya: You have been a resource, guide, and friend to me from my first phone screen in 2017 to date. You made moving to NYC easy for me because I knew I had someone to lean on whenever I needed to. You have always had my back and then some, both inside and outside of the office. Thank you for the work ethic, critical thinking, creativity, and strength you have instilled in me. I would not be the employee or person I am today without having a woman like you to look up to.

Tanya: You are magic in human form. The sappy goodbye card message I wrote to you as an intern in 2018 remains the same today: Our paths were meant to cross and I am so happy they did sooner in my lifetime than later. I attribute my ability to analyze the "follow-on effect" from actions in the workplace to my time working alongside you. Thank you for supporting me through every decision I have made even when that meant pivoting out of our team.

Lyons aka my favorite former professor: I am not sure what I did to deserve your continued support but am so thankful to have had it during my transition to New York and full-time employment. You have helped keep me grounded and sane during some of the most stressful times in my life. I appreciate your friendship, perspective on life, and honesty.

Mom and Dad: My successes are your successes because nine out of ten times you're right alongside me, helping me brainstorm ideas, moving me in or out of new cities, and cleaning up the pieces when I've made a mess. Thank you for encouraging me to never settle for anything less than adventure in this lifetime and always helping me achieve that.

Alex and Jeff: Being vulnerable enough to share your art with the world is extremely difficult. It takes a lot of bravery. I have always admired your dedication to your music careers, but after writing this book I can now appreciate your journeys in ways I couldn't before. I am so proud to be your sister and am very lucky to be able to say that my siblings double as two of my best friends. I love you and you constantly inspire me to be good.

Josh, Chris, Brian, and Michael: I cannot do this life without you. You keep me going. You are who I spend most of my time with, which is the only reason I've turned out OK because I reflect each of you back into the world. Sorry that you got the short end of the stick on that one by spending so much time with me!

Michelle, Alex, Katie, Kristina, and Nat: Thank you for being on the receiving end of every (probably drunk) venting session and putting the *life* in my work-life balance. You inspire me to speak my mind and stand up for myself and others. I am so thankful for all these years you have supported me without hesitation. I cherish the sparkle that your friendships bring to my life.

Patient T: You saw my potential long before I ever realized it was there. I appreciate how you have always encouraged me to become the best version of myself. My time working alongside you has significantly changed the trajectory of my career and life. The rest I'll save for the beer.

ABOUT THE AUTHOR

Brooke Carter is a young professional currently located in Seattle, Washington. She recently moved to the West Coast after three fabulous and fast-paced years of living in New York City.

Brooke spent the summers of her collegiate years establishing a track record of successful participation in summer internship programs of varying industries and job functions. Following her graduation from the University of Georgia in 2018 she immediately moved to the Big Apple, where she spent the foundational years of her career as a Junior Recruiter and Business Manager in FinTech. Her full-time career experience to date has been rooted in Junior Talent/University Recruitment as well as Business, Project, and Program Management for Global Data Science teams.

Her enthusiasm around her own career development extends

to that of family, friends, and strangers. She hopes that sharing a compilation of her experiences and favorite mantras will help others navigate their own post-collegiate transition into working full time. When she's not working, writing, online shopping, exercising, or talking her friends' ears off on FaceTime, you can find Brooke a few strong margaritas deep, eating at her favorite local vegan restaurants.

Today, Brooke works as a Program Manager of Machine Learning Education in Tech, a role and industry she never would have fathomed she was capable of pursuing until now. Her ACL, MCL, and meniscus are (slowly) on the mend, and she is thoroughly enjoying this new chapter of life she calls "Post-Profreshional Recovery."

Printed in Great Britain
by Amazon